Leaves
of
Truth

LEAVES OF TRUTH

Essie Pollion Luckett

VANTAGE PRESS
New York • Los Angeles

FIRST EDITION

All rights reserved, including the right of
reproduction in whole or in part in any form.

Copyright © 1990 by Essie Pollion Luckett

Published by Vantage Press, Inc.
516 West 34th Street, New York, New York 10001

Manufactured in the United States of America
ISBN: 0-533-08922-0

Library of Congress Catalog Card No.: 89-90585

1 2 3 4 5 6 7 8 9 0

Dedicated to
My

Devoted Husband	John Luckett, Sr.
Lovely Daughter & Son	M. Diane Luckett Holt John Luckett, Jr.
Mother & Father	Johnnie & Margaret Polliion
Aunt	Gieula Fly Benson
Super Niece & Nephew	Essie Pollion Jones William Pollion
Special Friend	Rev. Harold Chandler
Wonderful Cousin & Family	The Rt. Rev. E. Lynn Brown

Bishop Brown, you've always been there whenever I
needed you,
    To do for me whatever it was that I asked you to.
You're special to me and I want the whole world to know it,
    And in any way I possibly can, I'll always show it.
May God continue to bless and give you a long and fruitful
life,
    Not only you, Bishop, but your children and
        Gladys, your lovely wife.

A special
Thanks to Bishop William H. Graves
for his wonderful words of encouragement and also to
Dr. N. Charles Thomas

Acknowledgments to the College of Bishops of the
Christian Methodist Episcopal Church.
There are people who stick by you
    through thick or thin.
And it matters not to them whether
    you lose or win.

Three such people who have been a
    constant source of inspiration are:

    My friend and confidante, Melissa Conner Fox

    My sister-in-law who has become more like the sister
I never had, Edith Mae Pollion

    And another special cousin, Leroy Anderson

    I thank God for each of you.

Contents

Preface   xiii
Introduction   xv

Part One: Religious Poetry
A Gift from Heaven   3
My Life   4
If I Stumble   6
A Tribute to My Husband   7
Legacy to My Children   9
Mother   11
A Tribute to My Father   12
In Memory of My Late Mother-in-Law   14
My Dream   15
I'll Always Love You   17
My Love for You   18
How Much Do I Love You   19
True Love   20
Make Me Humble   21
A New Chance   22
A Dedicated Life   24
Youth   25
The Chains that Bound Me   27
The Church   29
Inner Peace   30
A Boy to his Mother   34
Train That Child   35
Who Am I?   37

Ruth (I) 38
Ruth (II) 40
An Invitation 40
Shades of Night 41
What Is a Father? 42
Looking for Peace 43
Be True 44
Why Are We Losing Our Youth? 46
The Handiwork of God 47
A Change of Heart 49
You Will See It Again 57
Lord, Give Me Faith 59
The Tongue 61
Peace 63
Classroom Angel 64
Walk with God 66
God Knows 67
Hatred 68
What Did You Do Today? 69
What Are Missionaries? 71
Stewardship 74
Be Grateful 77
Assurance 78
Keep the Faith 78
Why Doubt? 79
How Will You React? 81
Give Your Best 82
Share 83
Guide Me 84
The Harvest 84
Accept Whatever Comes 85
The Clock of Life 86
Hospitality 88
A Christian's Garden 89

Remember Your Promise 91
Lest I Forget 92
Negativism in the Church 93
A Glimpse of Heaven 95
A Gift from God 95
Christians Working for the
      Up-building of God's Kingdom 96
My Silent Partner 97
What Is Your Purpose in Life? 98
Christians in the Mainstream with Christ 99
So We Go Singing Onward 100
A Bridge Builder 101
It's Later than You Think 102
A Virtuous Woman 103
Somebody Cares 104
I Wonder 105
Why 106
My Prayer 107
Count the Cost 107
A Sinner Repents 108
I Know He's There 111
Death 113
Just Trust in God 113
Life's Crossroads 114
My Rendezvous with God 115
What Keeps Me Going 116
Father, Forgive Me 117
God's Masterpiece 117
No Peace 118
Don't Quit 119
I Prayed for You Today 120
An If for Christians 121
A Teacher's Prayer 122
A Great Experience 123

Peace Within 124
Check Your Life 125
A Job Transition 126
Mary's Grief 128
Easter 129
The Beauty of Easter 129
Guess Who 130
Suppose 130
Christmas (I) 131
Tired Elves 131
Christmas (II) 132
Try Smiling 133
Life (I) 134
Life (II) 134
Pleading 134
Smile 135
Love 135
Home 136
People 137
I've Learned to Be Content 138
What Is Life? 139
Daniel 141
All of Us Are Guilty 142
In Tune with God 144
Pseudo-Christianity 146
Dusk to Dawn 149
We Pass This Way Once 150
Thanksgiving 151
Consolation 152
In Times Like These 152
Thank You, God 153
Beyond the Horizon 157
Talent 158
A Good Layman 158
Be Patient 160

Part Two: Welcomes, Introductions, and Responses

Welcome (I)	165
Welcome (II)	165
Welcome (III)	166
Introducton of a Speaker (Woman)	167
Introduction of a Speaker (Man)	168
Response (I)	169
Response (II)	170

Part Three: Addresses

Check Your Heart Out	173
Take a Look at Your Insurance Coverage	175
Harvest Day	178
The Star of Bethlehem	180
Bethlehem's Star	185

Part Four: Tributes and Eulogies

A Tribute to Our Boss	189
A Tribute to Dr. Joyce Jenson	190
Service	192
A Job Well Done	193
This Is Your Life	194
A Tribute	195
A Farewell to Friends	195
Eulogy	197

Part Five: Miscellaneous Poetry

Listen to My Side	201
A Challenge—A Chance	203
February Rap	204
A Daily Challenge	205

Children   207
Don't Shed Tears for Me   208
Tennessee   209
The Beauty of Youth   211
Growing Old   211
Wonders of Nature   212
Snow   213
Snow Is Falling   213
Fall   214
March   215
The Beauty of Spring   216
Spring   217

Preface

It is with sincere gratitude and a deep sense of humility
that I write this book. At the request and persistence of
my friends and many acquaintances down through the
years, I have decided to share these writings and pray
that something herein will be an inspiration to someone
in some way.

It had been a tremendous inspiration to hear your
kind expressions of encouragement so many times. These
writings emerge from the very depths of my being
through the guidance of the Holy Spirit. If any portion
can be beneficial to any of my readers, I'll know and revel
in the thought that my effort has not been in vain. This
will be a great reward for me.

Thanks to each of you for helping to make this work
a reality, especially to the typists, Joan Bridges, Grace
Watson, Tammy Clark, and J. B. Morris.

May God bless you in a special way.

Introduction

When my mind went back across the corridors of my
history and I pitched a mental tent on the various
watersheds of my life, I discovered that I've always had
an insatiable desire for the truth as it related to the
ongoing unity of humanity. I have tried to express this
truth in a book of poetry and addresses entitled: *Leaves
of Truth*.

A tree, in my opinion, represents the family of
humanity. Its branches represent the various races of
humanity; and the leaves represent individuals of the
human race that are always subject to the many frailties
of life, which in itself is a given axiom—a universal truth.
I am deeply inspired by the words that fall from the pen
of an unknown author:

What a shaking thing
The truth can be
Especially when found
On a family tree.

John Alford was right when he asserted that truth
does not consist in minute accuracy of detail, but in
conveying a right impression; and there are vague ways
of speaking that are truer than strict facts would be.

John Hay Allison was certainly on target as it relates
to me and expresses my feelings in my poems and
addresses when he said, "Truth is the disciple of the
ascetic, the quest of the mystic, the faith of the simple,
the ransom of the weak, the standard of the righteous,
the doctrine of the meek and the challenge of Nature."
Together all of these constitute the Law of the Universe.

Thus—*Leaves of Truth*

Leaves
of
Truth

PART ONE

RELIGIOUS POETRY

A Gift from Heaven

(To our lovely daughter, Margaret Diane)

You were sent to us, darling, so
    clean and sweet,
From the top of your head to the
    sole of your feet.
To bring us joy in life and
    happiness and love
Just a sweet bundle of joy sent
    from above.
The happiness you've brought us is
    far beyond compare,
For you were so sweet and innocent
    and didn't have a care.
We've tended you carefully and
    watched you grow,
But what life holds for you,
    we just don't know.
You were always such a sweet
    and lovely child,
With heart so kind and mannerisms
    so calm and mild.
You were always obedient and did
    as you were told
And, darling, you mean more to us
    than silver or gold.
You've always been respectful to both
    your dad and me,
Even though there were things on which
    we didn't agree.
You're all grown up now and have
    children of your own,

But you've given us some of the greatest
        joy we've ever known.
I hope and pray that the life I've
        lived in front of you
Will inspire you to live just as
        Christ wants you to.
And that you'll instill in those darling daughters
        a sense of right
And will cling to the Saviour with
        all your might.
I thank God for you, darling, each and
        every day I live,
For you are one of the best gifts that
        Heaven could give.

My Life

I want to live so that when my time
        comes to go,
I won't have a saddened heart and
        head hung low.
I want to make the transition
        with great anticipation
Knowing that this is the joy of
        my Christian consummation.
I want to be able to put loved ones'
        minds at rest
And reassure them that Jesus helped me
        stand the test.
I want to be able to look at death with
        a smile on my face
And know, like Jesus, that I'm going
        to a better place.

I want to live so that others will want
        to emulate me
And in my daily life Jesus'
        teachings to see.
I want to leave a legacy of
        humility and love
For my friends and loved ones
        before going above.
I don't want to cringe from the icy
        fingers of death,
For I know it will be then that I'll
        inherit my wealth.
Jesus went on ahead in order to prepare
        a place for me,
So that throughout eternity, with
        Him I would be.
Even though old cunning Satan will
        make one last try
To win me over to his side before
        I come to die,
I'm striving to be rooted so deeply in
        Jesus' love then,
That it won't bother me a bit when
        this life comes to an end.

If I Stumble

If I stumble in this life, please
let it be uphill
And let it be for naught, dear God,
but trying to do Thy will.
Just give me the strength to rise,
tiresome though it may be.
Lord, help me to keep on climbing
and putting my trust in Thee.
If at times I criticize a fellowman,
let it be constructive and fair,
For it is my sincere desire to never
cause another worry or care.
Let me not speak hastily some thoughtless
word or do some unkindly deed
Nor place a stumbling block in a brother's way,
so he'll fail to succeed.
Help me that I will never hurt other
women, men, girls or boys,
But let me walk with them and talk with them
and share their sorrows and joys.
Let me not be envious of other's accomplishments
no matter how small or great,
But give me the patience to keep on climbing,
laboring and my turn to wait.

If I stumble in this life, please
let it be uphill.
Help me to keep on climbing and my
mission on earth fulfill.
Let me not become haughty no matter
how many material things I gain,
Help me to keep in mind that no matter
what it is, it all with time will wane.

Help me, dear God, to keep on climbing
though the hills get steep.
Just help me to get my balance and
over the obstacles safely creep.
Guide my footsteps as I climb
uphill from day to day,
So that I can evade the stumbling blocks
my enemies put in my way.
Help me to overcome the many pitfalls
of trouble and despair
Just guide me around them and
keep me ever aware
Of the goal that I'm striving so
very hard to attain
And continue to reassure me that
my stumbling will not be in vain.

A Tribute to My Husband

Many years have passed now since our vows were said,
    Many happy moments we've had—and many tears
have been shed.
Many roads were smooth, but many more were rough,
    But you always stuck by me when the going got tough.
You've loved me, reprimanded me, and taught me, my
dear;
    You've hidden your disappointments in order to give
me cheer.
You've prayed to God that our lives would be a guiding
light
    To inspire our darling children to do what is right;
And our friends also hoping that they too would find
    The kind of happiness we have and peace of mind.

II

When the honeymoon was over and our marriage really
began,
>   You've always stood tall and been the man
>   That I thought from the very first you would be,
>   And darling, that has meant the whole world to me.

When I was sick or cross or just plain mean,
>   You let me know that I had someone on whom to lean,
>   Someone who loved me and all my problems shared,
>   Who was kind and patient and always cared.

I trust as the years continue to pass and our love grows
older,
>   We'll love each other even more and to God become
closer.
>   And if I'm cut down today, you can always remember
this:
>   Marriages may not be made in Heaven,
>   But ours was truly one of bliss.

Legacy to My Children

Children, I can't leave you money or any great wealth,
    I can't give you the assurance that you'll have good
health.
    I can't promise you a pleasant and carefree life of ease,
    And I certainly can't promise that everyone in this
life you'll please.
    I can't promise you rubies or pearls and diamond
rings.
    In fact, not very many inexpensive material things.
    I can't promise you friends who'll stay by your side,
    Or even relatives in whom you can always confide.
    I can't assure you that you'll always be happy and gay
    As you go through this life from day to day.

But there is something that I can—and do—bequeath to
you,
    If you'll listen to Mama and do as she tells you to.
    I leave you a God whom I know really does care,
    And will each day of your life your troubles share.
    I leave to you the Bible, which is God's holy word
    And His beautiful promises that from me you've
heard.
    I leave you the assurance that He will never forsake
you.
    I leave you the comfort that He will hear and answer
your prayers
    And that to His Heavenly throne you'll both be heirs.
    I bequeath to you my capacity to forgive and forget,
    Like unto Jesus, the greatest man the world ever met.

I leave to you humility, happiness, and soberness of mind
    So that you'll try to inspire others this same joy to
find.

I leave you patience like unto Job of yesteryears
The kind that dispels your doubts and calms your
fears.
I leave you the desire for inner peace, which only
Christ can give
And a sincere desire to seek to always do His will.
I leave you honesty, which will keep your conscience
clear
Even when disappointments come and your enemies
are near.

Then I bequeath the greatest thing of all, which is love.
It will make you very wise and as harmless as a dove.
These bequests might seem naught to you children
today,
But use them wisely, for they'll take you home to
Heaven to stay.

Mother

Who is it who cared for me so many years,
Tended my scars and wiped away my tears,
Listened to my problems whether large or small,
Kissed away the sting of bruises, dirt and all,
Came to my rescue whenever I was in distress,
Whispering words of comfort whenever I was oppressed,
With the new things in life that I'd never faced before,
Forgiving my disobedience and loving me all the more,
For she had traveled the path over which I had to trod.
And she had love in her heart and faith in God.
Yes, Mother dear, it is of you whom I speak.
I'll always love and your wisdom I'll seek.
For a long time, Mother, I've tried hard to find
Some beautiful way to say what's on my mind
About the wonderful example you set for me
And the way you always clung to Calvary's tree.
Words seem to fail me and I can't really express
My thanks for your guidance and years of happiness
That you gave so freely with no thought of pay.
But I promise you, Mother, I'll make it up to you someday
By being the type of person that you've prayed I'd be.
And I'll do it too, Mother—just you wait and see.

A Tribute to My Father

Mom, I've given you lots of credit, but Daddy deserves
some too,
For he helped to shape our lives into what we'd do.

Dad, you have played a great big part in my life
And helped me when I grew up to become a good wife.

You proved you loved us even though you seldom said so,
But by the things you did, each of us had to know
That you cared and wanted us to be the best
And always told us that we would have to pass life's test.

Even though you didn't have the opportunity for a formal
education,
You were one of the hardest workers of your generation.

You taught us to be honest and work for what we got
And that being respectful to others would always mean
a lot.

You worked for years outside in the rain
With no sick days or retirement, yet you did not complain,
For you knew you had a wife and four children too.
And no one needed to tell you what you had to do
To feed and clothe us and also pay the rent,
For you knew that from Heaven it wouldn't be sent.

The total responsibility was yours and you always knew it
And even though you could have, you never blew it.

All you asked was that God give you the physical power
To do that hard manual labor hour after hour.

Very seldom was money on any foolishness spent
You didn't just talk but showed us what you meant
By working hard yourself each and every day
Even though you received a very little pay.

But you spread that little money so very far
To help each of us become, today, what we are.

We heard you pray and sing for years in a quartet,
For it seemed, some of your problems, it helped you forget.

We never saw you drink, we never heard you curse,
And the life we lived certainly could have been worse.
There were many good days and many happy nights
When we roasted potatoes by the dim lamp light.

Though things were not always easy, my childhood was
a happy one,
And admiration and respect from me you certainly won.

So may I say thanks a million times for you Dad,
Because for you to have been mine made me very glad.

In Memory of My Late Mother-in-Law

(MINNIE LEE HANNAH)

Your life on this earth is now ended,
    Your troubles will be no more;
You've now crossed the chasm
    Beyond the distant shore.
You've prayed your last prayer and
    Sung your last song,
You're through now giving up
    The right for the wrong.
You've paid the debt that each of us
    Too must pay,
And now you can rest until that
    Great judgment day.
All of us will miss you, Heaven
    Knows we will
And the void that you have left,
    No one else can fill.

But we thank God for letting you remain
    With us for many years
And though we are grateful,
    Parting still brings briny tears.
We have many pleasant memories
    To cherish from day to day,
But we'll miss the wisdom that
    You've shared along the way.
The awful pain that wracked your
    Body is now o'er,
And Jesus awaits to welcome you through
    An open door.

The love and respect I've had for you
    Will always remain in my heart,
For whatever I have accomplished in this life,
    You played a great part.
So sleep on, Mama Minnie, God knew
    You deserved the rest
And when it came to Mothers-in-Law,
    You were one of the best.

> Your Daughter-in-Law,
> Essie Pollion Luckett

My Dream

I had a wondeful dream one night while I slept,
One that I've carefully wrapped and hopefully kept
In the back of my mind way on top of a shelf,
For it was a terrific dream, all about myself.
I dreamed I loved my fellowman both young and old,
And that I helped wandering sheep find their way back
to the fold.
And the life I led was as radiant as a life could be,
For the whole world could see Christ living in me.

II

I dreamed that when friends mistreated me or let me down,
I looked at them and smiled and always stood my ground.
And said, "I forgive you, for you're not entirely to blame.
'Tis Old Satan who wants to cause us shame
And make us hate each other and fuss and fight,
For he just can't stand to see us do right."
I dreamed that I treated my enemies so kind that they came to say,
"Please forgive me for the wrong I did to you today.
For I know now, in doing wrong things to you,
I've hurt Christ deeply and wronged Him too."

III

I dreamed that I inspired love wherever there was hate
And urged sinners to seek Christ before it was too late.
I dreamed that men of all religious creeds and races
Were drawn together regardless of the color of their faces.
And the fellowship exhibited was really something to see,
And the world was at peace as it was always meant to be,
Filled with love and compassion one man for the other
And that all men were treated as if they were brothers.
Then the powers of Heaven smiled down on us with pleasure,
For the faith of God had in man had been restored in full measure.
This wonderful dream, for me, will someday come true
When I can correct the faults in me that I see in you.

I'll Always Love You

Darling, my love for you will never
    grow old,
It only gets sweeter and stronger as
    the years unfold.
The true unfaltering love that I
    have for you
Is stronger now than the day
    we said "I do."
Then, darling, I know in my heart
    you feel the same way,
From the way you've reciprocated
    day after day.
You've always looked out for me
    as I have for you,
And you've done so many nice things
    I never expected you to.
So as the years pass and our lives
    here we'll finish,
Come what may, my love for you
    will never diminish.

My Love for You

My love for you grows stronger as
each day goes by,
And it never occurred to me before
to question why.
But as my thoughts now turn to
why I do love you
And why to you only I'll
forever be true,
I think of all the little things
you've done for me,
Things so insignificant that
no one else can see,
Like calling me on the phone in
the middle of the day,
Or whispering "I love you" in
that special way.
It's the smile I get from you in
the midst of a crowd.
It's a certain nod you give me across
a room so proud.
It's the reassuring squeeze you give
while holding my hand,
And the trust you have in me making
not a single demand.
It's all of these little things
rolled into one
That will keep my love for you after
all is said and done.

How Much Do I Love You

You ask how much do I love you.
    Is there any way to measure

The whole wide world that is
    our very own treasure?

Can you measure the grains of sand
    that on the beaches lie?

Can you count the blades of grass or
    stars in the sky?

Can you count the trees throughout
    this great world of ours?

Can you even attempt to measure
    man's creative powers?

Then how can I tell you how much I
    love you, except to say

You are my joy, my love, my
    inspiration from day to day.

True Love

True love can endure so many things,
And does not ask in return anything.
It is patient, humble, thoughtful, and kind,
With consideration for others always in mind.
It is not puffed up or swelled with pride,
And it keeps humility always by its side.
Love keeps growing if it's for real,
And the whole world will know how you feel.
It will keep you going when you want to quit.
In spite of obstacles, you'll always do your bit.
Love will make you smile when you feel like crying,
When you get entangled with life's problems without
trying.
It will make you, your enemies forgive,
And do some good for someone every day you live.
It will give you strength you never knew you had
To meet life's situations whether good or bad.
Love won't allow you to scheme and plot
To take from your brother whatever he got
By working hard and doing what he should
To care for his family just as you could.
Love doesn't become jealous when others succeed,
But it is constantly trying to do a good deed.
Love is a small word with a very large meaning
And on uselessness, you'll never find it leaning.

Make Me Humble

Lord, make me humble as through
this world I go.

Let me not neglect anyone, be it
friend or foe.

Make me humble, Lord, I certainly can't
do it alone.

Even all of my striving could in no way
for my sins atone.

Make me ever conscious, Lord, of just
how helpless am I,

And without your grace, I'd have no one
on whom to rely.

When I think about it, I'm no more than
a bubble afloat

And realizing this, I know that I have
no reason to gloat

About anything that I think I might
be able to do,

For whatever it is I can do, I owe it all,
Lord, to you.

Make me humble, Lord, so I won't get
puffed up with pride,

But keep me in your care and let me
in your love abide.

Make me humble, Lord, so I can see
the needs of others.

Let me walk with them and work with them
as sisters and brothers.

Touch my life, Lord, and pride will raise
its ugly head no more,

So that one day You'll greet me somewhere
on that distant shore.

A New Chance

God has granted you a brand new
        year, my son,
And it's entirely up to you what you'll
        do with this one.
Will you make the same mistakes as you
        did the last
Or will you do your best to profit
        from the past?
The slate is clean and the very first
        mark is up to you,
The places you'll go or just whatever
        you decide to do.

You have another wonderful opportunity
        to try and do
The things that last year you somehow
        failed to do.
You now have a chance to do many things
        you left undone
And to do a little good each day
        to help someone.
You have a chance to go places that
        you did not go
And to learn so many things that
        you never knew before.
You have another chance to spread
        a little cheer
To get hold with yourself and
        to conquer fear.
To give your best in everything
        you do and say,
And take advantage of life's opportunities
        in every way.
You have a chance to scale the heights
        that you failed to gain
And achieve that goal that you
        did not attain.
He took the old year with all its
        cares and woes
And gave you a brand-new start
        midst friends and foes.
So it's up to you, my child, how
        you will use it
To accept with gratitude, go forward,
        or abuse it.

A Dedicated Life

I strive to keep both my body and mind clean and free
From all envy, hatred, strife, and all ungodly debris.

I strive daily to let everyone that I know
See Christ is with and within me wherever I go.

I don't put on airs and pretend to be what I am not
Or boast and brag to others about what I've got,

For whatever I have, it's because God gave it to me,
So I try hard to let the whole wide world see

That it makes me more humble the more I receive,
For this is the way God would have me be, I believe.

Christ had everything in this world that a king needed,
Yet, for the poor and down-trodden He often interceded.

I want to keep my thoughts on heavenly things above
And let my whole life radiate joy, peace, and love.

I want to inspire some wayward man, woman, girl or boy,
So they can realize living for Christ can be a real joy.

Let my conversation be centered around Godly things
And how trusting and believing in Him true happiness
brings.

Let me not be critical of others when mistakes they've
made
Even though their faults on the scale of justice are heavily
weighed.

Let me keep on marching 'mid turmoil, pain, and disaster,
Just keeping love in my heart and faith in the Master.

Youth

The whole world is disturbed
    about the plight of our youth,
Wondering why they are so arrogant
    disrespectful and uncouth.
But if you'll let your mind go back
    into the past for just a few years,
You'll remember our foreparents
    praying and shedding tears
And asking the same questions of the
    youth we're asking today—
"Tell me, young people, just why
    do you act this way?"
Well three-fourths of the trouble lies in us
    so let's be honest and face it
It won't fit anyplace else regardless
    of where we try to place it.
Sure, we give them plenty of food
    and lovely clothes to wear
And money in their pockets, but love and
    understanding are sort of rare
I mean the kind of love that makes us
    stand up for right and not give in
When we know what they are
    doing is a sin.
There are many other reasons why they
    shouldn't bear all the blame

For their many foolish escapades
        that cause immortal shame,
For if our lives were a guiding
        light for them to see,
They would, by our actions, know
        what their lives should be.
If we'd stop bickering among ourselves
        and running down each other
In their presence; forgive and forget
        then love one another;
If our morals were higher and
        our minds more stable,
Then and only then will we, their
        elders, be able
To correct them when we see
        them going astray
And with fairness but firmness speak
        to them in a God-fearing way
Then compel them to turn to Jesus in the
        prime of their lives,
And show them examples of other youth who
        did so and survived.
Then don't take that holier than
        thou and superior attitude
And put them down in front of
        their peers when they act rude
Because we too at one time were
        young and thought we knew everything
And stumbled along heedlessly till we
        realized only Jesus is king.
Then there are many other things today; dope and
        alcohol have been added to the devil's tools
To blow our youngsters' minds and
        make them act like fools,

So let's straighten up our lives and
      be that special light,
To guide them safely back into that
      shining path of right.
Their hearts are crying out for someone
      to help them find their way
Because they don't want to be lost
      regardless of what they say.
Let's help them to find the things
      in life they're searching for
Before their time comes to depart this
      life and cross the bar.
Let them know that life can be fun, but it
      has its serious side too
And remember, they won't hear what we're saying
      for watching what we do.

The Chains that Bound Me

There was a war going on inside of me,
'Til I accepted Christ and He set me free
Satan had me trapped and going his way.
He even intervened when I tried to pray.
There were times when I was happy as could be,
Then at times no one could get along with me.
For some reason I felt downhearted and defeated
When I was talked about and mistreated.
I didn't stop to think I might be on the right road
Just carrying what was my share of the load.
I'd read my Bible both day and night

While with old Satan I'd put up a fight,
Then I'd start out with new determination
And for a short time would be filled with elation,
But this feeling wouldn't last very long,
For all too soon something else would go wrong.
Then I'd just fall apart again and again
And find myself right back where I'd been.
The turmoil and pain kept me filled with doubt
And so many times I felt all washed out.
But one day I talked to God, just as I'm talking to you,
And pleaded with Him to show me what to do.
I turned my life over to Him that day
And said, Lord, take over and have your way.
He broke the chains that held me tight
And convinced me He loved me with all His might.
He took away doubt and replaced it with love divine
Assured me that I was His and He was mine.
When I really opened my heart, He came right in
Where, from that day to this, He has always been.
I hadn't realized He'd been standing there waiting
For me to invite Him in and stop debating.
I wasted so many days my own battles trying to fight
And convince others what they were doing wasn't right.
I'd even argued with them about what the Bible said,
Not realizing they knew, for they too had read,
But now I'm slow to anger and slow to speak,
For before I do, God's guidance I now seek.
I pray for those who dispitefully use me,
And no longer do I let them confuse me.

The Church

The Church is neglecting the job
      it was established to do
And God is holding us responsible
      yes, both me and you.
He said bear ye one another's burdens
      whether heavy or light
And love your neighbors
      with all your might.
He said take care of the widows and
      orphans from day to day,
Give your tithes, your talents,
      and watch and pray.
He said go to the highways and hedges
      and compel them to come,
But for some reason, very little
      of this is being done.
He said, "It is more blessed to give
      than it is to receive,"
But this is one statement that most
      of us just don't believe.
The Church is not set up
      to ostracize
Or look to find fault with
      others and criticize.
It's to be God-fearing, humble,
      peaceful and kind
With self out of the way
      and others in mind.
We're to be honest and fair
      in all our dealings
And even conscious of
      hurting other's feelings.

The Church is to speak boldly
      of Christ's teaching
And be sincere so that it
      will be far-reaching
To the dope addict, the drug dealer,
      and the prostitute
So that, from watching you, God's word
      they can't refute.
The Church just cannot with the world
      walk hand in hand,
For sooner or later you're going
      to be forced to take a stand.
You can't claim to be the Church and
      with Satan take sides,
For God's word lets us know that
      in no unclean place he resides.

Inner Peace

Through so many avenues I had
sought for peace,
But somehow from life's stress there
seemed no release.
I sometimes confided in friends and they
confided in me,
And for a while this did seem to help
to a degree.
I tried doing things—getting involved in
clubs and such,
But soon discovered that this didn't
help very much.

I had taught my children the very best
that I could,
And instilled in them the importance
of doing good.
I went to church from the time I
was a tot,
And from my Sunday school teachers I really
learned a lot,
But somehow there was always a void
inside of me,
An empty feeling that was surely not
meant to be.
I searched and searched, trying to find
peace of mind,
But the inner peace I needed, I couldn't
seem to find.
I went on methodically day after day
after empty day,
Doing what had to be done and feeling the
same old way.
Then in sheer desperation one day I
looked around
For the peace I'd sought so long but
couldn't be found.
Then as I walked down the street, I saw
this forlorn child,
Who from what I could see seemed to
be very wild.
Our eyes met for a long time as
we stood there.
And a voice within seemed to whisper, "He
needs your care."
He seemed drawn to me just as I
was to him.

And though there were others around, I
didn't see them.
It didn't come easy trying to reach
this confused little boy
And there were times when anything I said
seemed to annoy.
But I finally got him to open up to me
and occasionally smile.
He'd even began to come by the house and
visit for a while.
One of those rare occasions, his sad story
began to unfold,
And it was so very painful to listen
to what he told:
How his mother had died when he
was only four
And how, after that, his daddy just walked
out of the door.
How an old lady took him in, but in a
few years she died
And when he got to that part, he broke
down and cried.
"Why," he asked, "did God take her when He knew
she was all I had?"
According to him, from that very day, he
had turned bad.
He'd gotten into trouble by getting with
the wrong crowd
And by his own admission, he'd become
vulgar and loud.
He went on to say, "The old lady taught me about God's
love, you see
And how He would always take care of and
look out for me.

But from the day she died, it didn't
seem that way
Because nothing in my life has gone right
since that day.
Something strange happened though, when I
saw you that day
It's as if that dear old woman had sent
you my way."
It was then that I offered the lonely
boy a home
So, the streets no longer, he would
have to roam.
There was a shy smile on his face and his
eyes opened wide.
Then we quickly embraced and both
of us cried.
The feeling I had, at that moment,
deep down within,
Was the feeling of a long-time loser who
was about to win.
The inner peace I'd sought in so many
ways to find
Was attained so quickly by giving a wayward boy
peace of mind.

A Boy to His Mother

"Tell me, Mom, What is wrong
with me?
Why can't I be the boy you've
prayed I'd be?
You talked to me from the
time I was a tot
About how I should act and you
prayed a lot.
You read the Bible to me while
sitting on your knee
And told me what it said about the
way I should be.
You carried me to church and
to Sunday school.
It was there that I learned
the Golden Rule.
You watch and pray when I
am out at night
And I know that you love me
with all your might
But, Mom, the more you talk
the more I disobey.
I'm all confused, for I don't
want to be this way.
Mom, I love you even though I
don't show it.
It seems that every time I try to change,
I somehow blow it.
It tears me apart when I see
that you've been crying
Because you caught me misbehaving
and lying.

It's just like a dagger being
stuck through me
Because why I'm hurting you
I just can't see.
Some nights my pillow, too, is
wet with tears,
Thinking about the grief I've caused
you down through the years,
But last night I got down
on my knees,
And asked God to change
my ways please
And, Mom, somehow I just believe
He heard my plea,
And a different attitude you're
going to see in me."

Train That Child

Yes, that's your child, God gave him/her to you,
But, in his word, He also commanded you what to do.

He said, "Train up a child in the way he should go
And when he is old, from his training he won't go."

But you must begin from the time he's a tot
Because as he grows, peer pressure will mean a lot.

You can't let up because a few tears he'll cry.
'Tis far better to wipe the tears than to watch him die

By the hands of some gang of which he's become a part
Because once he's grown up, it's just too late to start

Chastising him and trying to make him do
The things as a little one you should have made him do.

Many books have been written on this subject, I know,
But the Book of Books spells out the way we should go

And, if you disregard what the Bible has to say,
Without a doubt, you'll regret it all some day

Children want to be disciplined if it's done in the right
way,
For they become confused if you are promiscuous day after
day.

They need guidance and you as a parent should know it
And if you truly love that child, you will surely show it

By having rules that they can understand and obey.
If you want them to grow up productive, that's the only
way.

Sure, there are exceptions to every rule under the sun,
But just be sure that you're not guilty of not doing
        All you should have done.

Who Am I?

I asked myself, "Who am I that God should care
If I have food to eat and clothes to wear?
That I should be protected from storm and rain,
That my sins should be forgiven again and again;
That I should be comforted when in distress.
Even when of my life I've made such a mess,
When I've lied and cheated and strayed from the fold,
When I've forgotten His goodness in my lust for gold.

Who am I that a great God should care
And help me daily all my crosses to bear?
When I've mistreated my sister and despised my brother,
Scorned my father and burdened my mother,
Ignored my friends when they were in despair,
Neither offering them food to eat or clothes to wear,
Just enjoying myself and looking out for me,
Regardless of circumstances all around I see."

Then, like a bolt of thunder, it came out of the blue,
A voice seemed to say, "Because God loves you,
In spite of all the wrong things you've done,
New hope was given when He sent His son.
You are the masterpiece of His greatest plan,
You're just a little lower than angels—you are man!"
So I know now who I am that God cares so much.
He hopes that someday my sin-sick soul He can touch.

Ruth (I)

(Taken from the Bible)

Ruth was a beautiful woman as the whole world could see,
Whose love for her mother-in-law certainly made history.

She left, not only her family, but her country and
everything,
So that she could be with Naomi and closely to her cling.

Ruth, no doubt, loved this woman so very much
And in a special way her life Naomi had to touch.

Ruth begged so earnestly for Naomi not to send her away
That Naomi was truly convinced that Ruth wanted to stay

Near her wherever she went midst friend or foe.
It was love that compelled Ruth to go wherever Naomi
would go.

She was willing to lodge wherever Naomi had to stay
And was also willing to care for her day after day.

She was not, as one poet described, just a phantom of
delight
But the epitome of beauty who loved Naomi with all her
might.

Ruth, the foreigner, in spite of the national boundary
lines,
Stood on loyalty, which, in the end, made her life sublime.

She commanded the respect of all who gazed upon her
beauty
Without even trying, for she was only doing a faithful
daughter's duty.

Ruth faced racial prejudice and religious animosity so
great,
But in spite of it she overcame, not daring to hate.

She gleaned food in the fields of Boaz, a rich Hebrew man,
And his charge to "touch her not" was not a request but
a demand.

Her sweet, humble, and gentle spirit was something to
see,
And immediately Boaz knew that his wife she'd some day
be.

So, in time, they married and God blessed them with a
son, Obed,
And it seems that Ruth to this country by God was surely
led.

Ruth (II)

R is for responsibility she felt
    for Naomi so strong;

U is for the unselfishness that to
    her did belong.

T is for the truth she spoke as she
    pleaded with Naomi that day,

H is for the humbleness that
    carried her a long way.

Put them together and they
spell Ruth—

A Moabite maiden who won with
love and truth.

An Invitation

Come, dear ones, come to the peace table,
Come now and worship while you are able,
Come with rejoicing and come with singing,
Come join in while joy bells are ringing.

Come just as you are, no fault in you we'll find,
For a more beautiful fellowship nowhere you'll find.
Come if you are young, come if you are old,
Come and help us Christ's name to uphold.

Don't hold back your tears, your joys or sorrow
For today is just a preview of what we'll share tomorrow.
We're so glad you've come and we hope you will stay
Pray with us and worship with us throughout this holy
day.

Shades of Night

When daylight is passed and shades of night so softly
appear,
I like to lie down to rest and look back over a day of cheer.
Not cheer in the sense of pleasure, good times, and fun,
But joy in knowing that I have helped someone;
Maybe it was a kind word or a very small deed
That helped someone who was sorely in need
Of the comfort I could give or the spirit I could brighten,
The smile I could bring and the load I could lighten.

When the daylight is passed and shades of night appear,
I don't want to lie restless because of fear.
Fear that I missed my chance to serve mankind;
For if I did, this chance I might never again find.
Fear that I might have caused someone to go astray,
To walk unheedingly in their own willful way.
Or to fail to do something that would have helped
someone,
Something that I could very easily have done.
Fear that the shadows of life might tonight close in and
find me
Unprepared to meet my Maker and with Him spend
eternity.

What Is a Father?

A father is the one who's there whenever he is needed
To comfort you when you fail and praise you when you've
succeeded.

To give a helping hand when on him you have to call,
To catch you with his strong arms when you're about to
fall.

He's firm but fair and loves you with all his might
And will chastise you, for he wants you to do right.

A father is one who constantly looks out for you
In sickness, in health, and in whatever you do

He looks out for his family with so much pride,
And oftentimes his troubles will in no one but God confide.

He goes his limit in sunshine or stormy weather
To keep things going and to keep his family together.

He'll do without so his wife and children can get,
Even if it means getting way overhead in debt.

He carries himself daily in such a Christian way
That love radiates from his life day after day.

He shares your joys and your disappointments too
And gives sound advice whenever you ask him to.

He doesn't always chatter and have so much to say,
For being very talkative just isn't his way.

A father is one who takes on an active part in your life
And tries hard to protect you from its troubles and strife.

He speaks with authority in so many little ways
That everyone in the household knows he means what
he says.

I guess you could sum it all up by saying on this Father's
Day
That a father is out front leading the way.

So to all the fathers in attendance here, may I say
God bless and keep you in His care from day to day.

Looking for Peace

If peace on this earth you ever hope to find,
There are some things you'll need to keep in mind.
Peace is not gained by having lots of material things,
Mink coats, beautiful name-brand clothes, and diamond
rings.
It doesn't come from having a fine home and expensive car,
A spacious home, custom drapes, and a great big bar.
It doesn't come from people who are in high places
Or trying hard to get ahead in life's rat races.
It doesn't come from friends, for they will let you down.
It doesn't come from praises, no matter how good they
sound.
It doesn't come from children, for they'll grow up and
leave you,

And in between, there'll be plenty of times they'll grieve
you.
It doesn't come from parents, though they love you so dear,
For their lives are oftentimes filled with confusion and
fear.
It doesn't come from the minister, efficient though he may
be,
For remember, he has problems the same as you and me.
It doesn't come from fortune as many will attest,
For many have attained fortunes but in them find no rest.
It doesn't come from fame no matter what the
contributions are,
For many famous people are the loneliest by far.
No. Real peace can come only within from deep down
inside
When you just open your heart to Christ and let Him
there abide.

Be True

In all things be faithful, in
all things be true,
In all things be honest, for
God is watching you.
You may be able to fool people as
through this life you go,
But it is a proven fact that you
will reap just what you sow.
Be just in all your dealings with
everyone you meet,

And never ever try others' good
works and deeds to defeat.
Be creative, God gave you a mind,
so don't fail to use it.
Be thankful in all things and
never neglect or abuse it.
Exercise your talents whether
they are many or few,
And worry not about others' abilities,
just do well what you can do.
Tell of God's goodness every chance
you get and wherever you go,
Just be yourself, for when you're
sincere, others will know.
Don't make apologies unless you
feel that they're really needed,
For most people failed again and again
before they succeeded.
Give of yourself to others as much
as you can possibly give,
And be determined to live the very
best life that you can live.
Love with a love that will reflect
Christ living in you,
And that love in great measure will
be given back to you.

Why Are We Losing Our Youth?

We seem to be losing our youth,
is a statement we often hear,
But if we are losing them, the
reason is certainly clear.
We let them tell us what they are
and are not going to do
From the time they are tots even
as young as two.
When they begin to throw their temper
tantrums, we back down,
Instead of nipping it in the bud
and standing our ground.
We think it's cute when they hit back,
scream and pout,
And by this time, why we're even
ashamed to take them out
Into public places where other
people will be able to see,
How awful your child can act and
how ashamed you'll be.
They see you drink, watch dirty movies,
hear you curse and swear,
And you'll let them do just about anything to
keep them out of your hair.
You give them whatever they want
no matter what the cost,
And by this time, all respect
for you is lost.
Young people want discipline, tempered
with love, the pair.
When it is, they don't have to wonder,
they know that you care.

So love them, yes, but teach them
almost from birth
To have honesty, respect for others,
and also self-worth.
Instill all of these virtues within
them each and every day,
Then show them by precept and
example what is the right way.

The Handiwork of God

Have you ever really taken a good look
        at this beautiful world God made,
How He bade the powerful mountains rise
        and the lovely plains He laid,
How the flowers and trees burst in bloom
        only when their time is set,
And how the beautiful grass comes forth
        and with the morning dew is wet,
How He can speak to the wind and
        it will cease to blow
Or give orders to the elements to send
        forth rain, sleet, or snow?

Have you ever stood and gazed at the skies
        with clouds of different array
Then closed your eyes in sleep and
        awakened to another wonderful day
And watch the sun out of the east appear
        then travel on to the west,
Where it will no longer be seen that day,
        for the time has come for it to set.

Have you really stood and watched the lightning
    flickering boldly across the sky
Or taken the time to listen to the thunder
    as it roared fiercely by?

Have you ever driven along the highway
    and watched the ocean blue
Or watched the peaceful sand-filled beaches
    that just seem to beckon you?
Have you ever watched soft white snowflakes
    as they so gently fall
Or listened in awe to the sound
    of a whippoorwill's lonely call?
Have you ever walked through a forest
    with its wide assortment of trees
And carefully approached a hive where
    honey is made by bees?

We take all this beauty for granted
    without giving a single thought
To the undeniable fact that it could
    only by our God be wrought.
So slow down your pace and take
    full advantage of the view.
It's all there for us, for God made it
    just for me and you.
The world has produced many artists
    all down through the ages
Some of whom, though by any standards great
    yet, never made history's pages.
Many left footprints on the sands of time
    as through this world they trod,
But no artist, neither living nor dead,
    could emulate the handiwork of God.

A Change of Heart

I'd taken God's blessings with a selfish
 and arrogant air
And for all of His goodness, I'd never
 offered a prayer.
I walked on so many people in order to
 obtain what I got
Because the material things of this world,
 to me, meant a lot.
I gave no thought to others who were less
 fortunate than I.
It never dawned on me that one day
 I had to die.
I had a beautiful wife and daughter and
 handsome son too,
And I was so wrapped up in them I didn't
 know what to do.
I'd given my children everything they needed
 except guidance and care.
What was more important to me was name-
 brand clothes to wear.
Everyone looked up to me as someone great
 to be admired,
But they didn't know that at times I
 was troubled inside.
Then one day fate intervened and raised
 its terrible head.
A strange voice on the phone was saying, "We think
 your son is dead."
And my lovely daughter seemed to be right
 at death's door.
I stood there telling my wife and
 she paced the floor.

It was the new car I'd given him only yesterday
    with so much pride,
And it was I who had persuaded them to
    go for that ride.
I wanted them to let the entire
    neighorhood see
That expensive and beautiful car given
    to him by me.
My daughter didn't want to go—said she
    just wanted to be alone,
And her words flashed before me as I
    stared at the phone.
No, no, dear God, please, God, don't
    let this be true.
I'll do anything on earth that you
    want me to do.
Give my son back, dear God, and please
    spare my daughter's life
And we'll do your will—not only me
    but also my wife.
Then out of the depth of my mind
    a sobering answer came;
All of your adult life, you have failed
    to call His name.
I thought of how I'd gone to church with my
    mother every Sunday,
But once I grew up, it all seemed so
    ridiculous and funny.
I'd always told my children they could go
    if they wanted to,
But most of the time we just had
    so much to do.
I remembered how, at times, my daughter pleaded
    "Let's go to church today.

I like to hear the minister preach and
	hear the deacons pray."
I'd say, "Okay, honey, we'll go," but really I
	never gave it a thought.
Like everything else, I thought our way to
	Heaven could be bought.
I can remember her face being radiant just a
	few Sundays past,
When she called us together and said she'd
	found Jesus at last.
I smiled, her brother shrugged, and my
	wife just gave a nod,
For by now we'd long since forgotten
	there was really a God.
Then that something that had troubled me
	inside seemed to say,
That's what Mary was trying so hard to
	tell us that day.
Then my wife's screams seemed to
	penetrate my being
And the ungrateful people we'd become I, for the
	first time was seeing.
Then we embraced and both of us
	fell on our knees to pray,
But both of us, at this time, were lost
	for words to say.
Then my mind rushed back to childhood
	at my mother's knee.
I can hear her saying now, "I want you
	to repeat after me."
The prayer seemed long and I would
	soon get tired,
But there was always a peaceful look on
	her face that I admired.

I can remember some parts that I
    think went like this,
Some of it I still remember, but some
    I know I'll miss
It began, "Our Father who art in Heaven
    hallowed be thy name."
Dear God, I can't remember what's next, but
    I know I'm to blame.
My wife and I stayed there for what
    seemed an eternity,
Just lifting our hearts and hands to Him
    in an earnest plea.
After a while strength seemed to come
    from out of nowhere.
Then we rushed to the hospital because
    our children were there.
Though the hospital was close, right now,
    it seemed so far away,
And as we drove along the streets, I
    never ceased to pray.
As soon as we entered, the doctor
    met us at the door
And said, "Your daughter is in intensive care
    on the second floor.
It doesn't look too good and she's been
    asking for both of you
And she keeps on saying there is something
    the two of you must do."
Then I heard my wife's faint voice ask,
    "What about our son?"
"His condition is stable, the toughest part
    for him we've won."
So somehow we followed the doctor
    to the second floor

And our daughter smiled faintly as
        we walked through the door.
She immediately started talking and we thought
        she was out of her head
And trying hard to tell us that her
        only brother was dead.
She reached out her hand to me
        and to her mother.
"Come closer, Mom and Dad, there's something you
        must do for each other."
We interrupted to tell her that our
        John was still alive
And all that we were praying for now
        was for her to survive.
She motioned us to be quiet and listen
        to what she had to say,
For she was going home to be with
        her God today,
"But there is something I must tell both of
        you before I leave,
Repent of your sins, accept Christ in your
        hearts and believe.
It's not too late, He's standing at your
        heart's door pleading
And with His father, on your behalf
        He is interceding.
God will forgive you for everything
        wrong you've done.
That was proven years ago when God
        sent us His son
To die on the cross that day
        on Calvary's rugged tree.
So that one day all of us could
        with Him be.

He's given you, Mom and Dad and John
        another chance to do
The things on earth that the Bible
        commanded you."
The doctor who stood quietly listening said,
        "That's enough for now,"
But Mary whispered, "It's all right, doctor, I'll
        be leaving soon anyhow.
You see I asked God to take me and
        leave John here
And let his story be one for the
        whole world to hear,
For you see John accepted Jesus while
        we were riding along
As I was singing to him what I call
        my favorite song.
When I got to the part about earth has no
        sorrow Heaven cannot heal,
He joined in and told me how good inside
        he began to feel.
Then he said, 'I thank you, Mary, and
        I thank God too
For giving me a lovely Christian
        sister like you.'
It was at that very moment the other
        car ran a light.
John held on and struggled with
        all of his might
And the last thing I can remember was
        hearing John pray
'Please, dear God,' he said, 'don't take
        my sister away.'
I held John's head and told him
        not to worry, you see.

'It's just God's way of letting us know
      He's ready for me.'
So, Mom and Dad, I know John is
      going to be all right.
My Heavenly father revealed that to me while
      lying here tonight.
It's you that I'm praying for to
      change your life-style.
The material things you have will
      only last for a while.
Promise me you'll do that right
      here and now.
Jesus is still pleading and He knows
      your hearts anyhow.
So stop crying, Mom, and don't look
      so lonely, Dad.
I'm going home to live with God and
      I am so very glad."
As we leaned over her, she kissed each
      of us on the cheek
And we could tell that she quickly was
      getting very weak.
Another angelic smile crossed her
      thin but beautiful face
And somewhere in the distance I
      remembered Amazing Grace.
Her hand gripped ours tightly for just
      a short little minute,
But that grip Mary gave truly had
      something in it.
When the doctor rushed to her side and took
      out his stethoscope
Then sadly shook his head, we knew
      there was no hope.

I suddenly had the strangest feeling
        that I'd ever had.
Said the doctor, "Meeting Mary has somehow
        made my heart glad.
I feel that her sweet presence will
        always be here."
And in that doctor's eye, I could
        see a tear.
We went on to John to see how he
        was getting along,
And as we entered the room, he was
        singing this song:
"Pass me not, O gentle Saviour, won't
        you hear my plea,
Help my Mom and Dad to dedicate
        their lives to Thee."
Then he searched our faces and
        so softly cried,
For he could tell from our looks that
        his sister had died.
We both kneeled down right there beside
        John's hospital bed,
And I know now that Jesus listened to
        every word we said.
Our prayer was that God would deliver us
        that very night
And help us to do only what was pleasing
        in His sight.
He didn't hesitate either but just
        stepped right in
And put love in our hearts where
        greed had been.
God had spared our son and we
        were so very proud

That we could be heard down the hall
        singing His praises aloud.
In a hospital on that day, we
        started out anew
Doing the things Mary and God
        had helped us to.
Our entire lives now experienced
        a total revolution
And established within our hearts
        a wonderful institution.
Many times old Satan tries so hard
        to turn us around,
But we rebuke him in Jesus' name, for
        we are Heaven-bound.
So now the pain of losing Mary
        isn't so hard to bear,
For we know she's with God and
        safely in his care.

You Will See It Again

You can stir up trouble as through
this life you go,
And think you're getting by and that
no one else will know
About the mean little tricks and snide
remarks you make
And the name of the Lord, in vain
you often times take.
You can break other folks' hearts and
cause them unhappiness

And heap on problems when they're
already in distress.
You may stick a dagger in the back
of a fellowman,
But belive it or not, my friend, you're going
to see it again.

You might go on a long time cheating,
lying and stealing,
And a friend's problems go all over
the neighborhood revealing.
You can laugh and point a finger at others less
fortunate than you,
And fail to do for the needy whatever
good you can do.
You can use that vicious tongue to spread
hatred and lies,
And ignore the pitiful pleading of a
hungry child's cries.
You can preach your heart out and not live
what you are preaching.
You can be the world's greatest teacher and not
live what you are teaching
You can live a lifetime doing all the
mean things you can,
But according to the Bible, my friend, you
will see it all again.

Then you can do good for others who do
evil to you,
And keep on doing right regardless of
what they do.
You can visit the imprisoned, the destitute,
the sick and the old.

You can go on doing your best, Jesus Christ's
teachings to uphold.
You can forgive others who have done
wrong to you
And do, to your best ability, what the Bible
tells you to.
You can pray for others even when they
are doing you wrong
And hold on to God's hand, for He
will make you strong.
If you cast your bread upon the waters by
helping your fellowman,
Without a doubt, in this life, you will
certainly see it all again.

Lord, Give Me Faith

Lord, give me more faith as I
walk this road,
Enough that I might help to
bear others' load.
The kind of faith that leaves
no room for doubt
Even when the worst of times in
life come about.
Give me an unwavering faith that
I'll be able to stand
And continue to walk with You
daily hand in hand.
I want that steadfast faith
that will carry me

Wherever You want me to go
o'er land or sea.
Lord, give me that unfaltering faith,
rooted and grounded in you
So that I'll be willing to do whatever you
assign my hands to do.
The kind of faith that shines
through clouds of doubt
Even when by loved ones and friends
I've been left out.
Lord, give me the kind of faith
that Job had of old
That will keep me going though I
buckle under the load.
The kind of faith exemplified by
Abraham that day
When he was willing on the altar
his son to lay.
The kind of faith that grows the
more it is used
Even when, for no reason, I've
been falsely accused.
Lord, give me the kind of faith that'll
help me stand my ground
Even though others retreat and
no one else is around.
The kind of faith that will make
me stand up for right
Even though Satan is pushing
with all his might.
I want the kind of faith that shines
through the darkest hour
And I'll know You're standing in the wings
with your saving power.

The Tongue

The tongue is a deadly, scheming, and
driving force,
Which has thrown many a person completely
off course.
It has caused many a sad heart
to bleed,
It has caused many a person not
to succeed.
It has caused many a friend to become
a foe
By talking about something of which you
did not know.
It has caused many a quarrel and
many a pain.
It has caused many a person's character
to be slain.
It has caused many a downfall and
many a tear.
It has crushed so many spirits and caused
so much fear.
It has caused entire families to be
torn apart.
It can be just like a dagger stuck
into the heart.
It has broken up companies and
corporations too
And had people so confused they didn't know
what to do.
It's really the most vicious part of the body
that we possess,
And causes so much chaos, trouble,
and unhappiness.

It has caused people lots of misery, grief,
and even hate,
It has caused many married couples to lose a mate
It has caused doubt many times where there
should be trust.
It has caused many an innocent person
to turn to lust.
It has caused people to do so many
mean things,
From tiny playmates, to teenagers, adults and
even kings.
It has caused dissension among both
young and old.
It has caused weak Christians to stray
from the fold.
I could go on and on talking of the evils
a tongue can do.
Search yourself to see if this is a clear
description of you.
Of course it doesn't just have to
be that way
If each of us would the golden
rule obey
And ask God to bridle our tongue each and
every day
And guide our thoughts toward good in whatever
we do and say.

Peace

Peace to different people means so many things
    walking along the beach
    soft clouds just out of reach
A beautiful robin on the wing.
A comfortable home to shelter us from the cold
    shiny faces of little tots
    people around us who mean a lot.
Loved ones to care for us when we get old.
A beautiful sunset in the western sky
    calm seas of azure blue
    knowing that God watches over you.
A friend on whom we can always care
The assurance that God will always rely
    come storm or sunshine from day to day
    in spite of trials encountered along the way.
He will all of our problems daily share.
To see peace on the face of a fellowman
    when he has given up hope
    while walking life's tight rope
When I go to his rescue and do what I can.
To watch the withered grass turn from brown to green
    the flowers with blooms come alive
    to know that a sick child will survive
To become aware of beauty you've never seen
    in the birds and the bees
    the shrubbery and the trees
And know what peace within really means.

Classroom Angel

(Inspired by a little girl named Paulette,
Celeste Mason Ontyl, and hundreds of
sweet children whose lives I touched.)

She came to my class, a quiet
and timid child,
With spirit so humble and
manner so mild.
She sat and listened attentively
day after day,
But unless she was coaxed, had very
little to say.
She watched my actions and
heard me scold
And undertook her tasks just as
she was told.
She had a contagious smile that
seemed divinely sent,
And she carried that smile
wherever she went.
Her scholastic record wasn't the
best I'd seen,
Even though she was observant and her
wits were keen.
Her concern for her peers was
genuine and sincere,
And the innocence she reflected
was refreshing and dear.
I never saw or even heard of her
doing things mean.
She was just one of the sweetest children
I'd ever seen.

She was loved by her classmates even though
she was shy,
And never, if questioned about things,
would she lie.
She shared with others both the
girls and boys,
And always exhibited a great
amount of poise.
Many times when I seemed engulfed
with frustration,
A look at that angelic face gave me
the inspiration
I needed so desperately to get through
the day
Even though she had not a word
to say.
Working with this child was such a
great pleasure
That the true value of its worth, one
could not measure.
I've watched this child since from my
class she's gone
And whether it was in a crowd
or all alone
That inward beauty, possessed by her,
was still there
As anyone around her will soon
become aware.
If some of that love and tranquility from her
could be captured
And spread, that the world by it might
be enraptured,
Real love and concern, for others, we
would never lack,
And all of us would be ready when
Christ comes back.

Walk with God

Try walking with God, but let
Him do the leading.
Let Him fight your battles without
your interceding.
Be quiet and listen, for He still
speaks to us,
But His voice we cannot hear mid
turmoil and fuss.
Let Him guide your thoughts each
and every day
What you think and the words
that you say.
Invite Him in on those great
plans you're making.
His advice is always there and
it's yours for the taking.
You never have to walk alone as
through life you go.
This is a fact that every child
of God should know.
Lean on Him and don't be afraid,
for He can take it
And will reassure you that with His
help you can make it.
Trust in Him, for He has never been
known to deceive,
But many trusting souls He
did gladly relieve.
Believe in Him sincerely with
all of your heart
And have no doubts, for He's
Almighty God.

God Knows

He can see through that deceitful smile to
that mean frown inside,
Try as you will that selfish and
despicable attitude to hide.
He can see through these shallow promises
that you knew you wouldn't keep
To the bad seeds sown that someday
you're sure to reap.
He can see the hatred that inside you've
harbored for so long,
That it's really hard for you now to
tell right from wrong.
He can see the jealousy that has your
mind so twisted and torn
In spite of the holy attire that on
Sundays you adorn.
He can see the envy you have for
some of your fellowmen.
He knows in which direction you're going.
He knows where you've been.
He knows the heartache you've caused as
along this life you went.
He knows the turmoil you started and
every bad vibe you've sent
Into the heart of another person even
when he was already depressed.
How with bitterness and wrongdoing
you seemed to be obsessed.
He knows when you're backbiting
and throwing stumbling blocks in the way.
He also knows that for these ungodly acts
you'll sooner or later have to pay
So you can either go on doing wrong or you can

clean up your act,
But that you'll reap what you sow is not
fiction but a proven fact.

Hatred

Hatred is like a cancer that's in
its very last stage,
And it is no respecter of persons'
creed, gender, or age.
It can eat away at the hater
to the very core,
And cause you to forget about
the cross that Jesus bore.
It can make you lose sight of
what is right and good
And create all kinds of problems
in any neighborhood.
Hate will cause you to try and
get even at any cost.
It can, if you let it, cause your
very soul to be lost.
It can distort your personality
and destroy your mind.
It can make you look for evil
in everyone you find.
It will make you lose faith in mankind
and start you to drinking.
It can cause you to distrust even
your very best friend,
And make you ignore him when the

friendship he tries to mend.
It can cause you to be suspicious of
everything and everyone,
And make you lose many a battle that
you should have won.
It will sap the very life out of
you every single day
If you don't come to yourself and
kneel and pray.
Hatred is one of the most dreaded
diseases that I know
One that will haunt you day and night
Wherever you go.
So ask yourself, "Is it really worth
all the inward pain?"
Or should you turn to Christ and
eternal life gain.

What Did You Do Today?

Did you stop to say, "Thank you, God,"
as you climbed out of bed
Or did you rush out thinking only of
how you could get ahead?
Did it cross your mind who'd watched
over you through the night
And protected you from harm and danger
from dusk to light.
Did you invite Jesus to ride with you
as you climbed into your car
And go the whole day long with you
no matter how far.

Did you ask Him to stay with you on
the job hour after hour
And to fill and sustain you with
His Holy power.
Did you give a full day's work as
you'd agreed to do
Or did you just goof off because the
boss wasn't watching you.
Did you treat those you encountered
with honesty and respect
And did you for just a while on
God's goodness reflect.
Did you give a smile to someone
who might've been low
Or give a gentle pat on the head of a
child you didn't know.
Then did you finish the day's work
all filled up with pride,
Thinking what a great job you'd done and
on no one else you'd relied.
Did you hurry out to your car not
offering anyone a ride
With empty seats in back and
front at your side.
Did you then rush home to your children
or husband or wife
To whom you've given many material
things in life.
Did each of you sit at the table in
your respective place
And enjoy that sumptuous meal
without a word of grace.
Dinner over, you watch TV and
then prepare for bed.

Not a word of thanks to God was given
not a single prayer was said.
Suppose God treated you like you treated
Him day out and in.
Just ask yourself, "Without Him what
would my life have been?"

What Are Missionaries?

Missionaries are the ones who
will strive to do
The things in this life that God
has commanded them to.
They look after the widows and orphans
both young and old,
And when it comes to witnessing for Christ
are very bold.
They're humble and steadfast just
as the Bible says
And their lives reflect it in hundreds
of ways.

They're not puffed up with pride but
meek and kind
With the welfare of others always
uppermost in mind.
They are always giving instead of
looking to receive
And a fellowman in distress, they're

always trying to relieve.
They pray for the success of the Church
both night and day
And carry themselves constantly in
a Christlike way.

They pray for the people who have
despitefully used them
And even, if given a chance, would in
no way abuse them.
They'll feed the hungry, visit the prison bound,
and pray for the weak
And each day of their lives God's
divine guidance seek.
They don't give up just because
the going gets rough
But hang in there until God says to
them "That's enough."

They'll go in the snow, the sleet
the sunshine or rain.
They'll go when their bodies
are racked with pain.
They are slow to anger and
are quick to forgive,
For they know this is the way that Christ
would have us live.
They seek not to be served but
rather to serve
And give every human being the
respect he deserves.

They let their lights shine always
both night and day
So some lost soul will be able
to find the way.
They oftentimes don't have degrees ot
even a formal education,
But what is much more important
is sincere dedication.
They don't get angry and decide to
go home and stay,
For they realize that there will
be a reckoning day.

They always speak encouraging words
to others in doubt
And reassure them that God already
has a way figured out.
Missionaries bridle their tongues, they
watch as well as pray
And they think and weigh their words before
they have anything to say.
They don't look for recognition, they
don't want praise.
They serve God through their fellowman,
for they know this is what pays
And will assure them a home with our
heavenly Father above,
Because their lives and works have
reflected God's love.

Stewardship

Give of yourself freely—your money,
    your talent, your time,
To enhance God's work here on earth
    involving all mankind.
Plan what you'll do to help someone
    every single day
Then bow down on your knees before
    God and sincerely pray.

Pay your tithes and offerings as He
    has said you should,
For in His word He promised He'd not
    withhold any good.
If this commandment you would
    follow to the letter,
There's no doubt in my mind that
    your life would be better.

Let your giving be freely, for He dosen't
    want it in a grudging way,
And lay not up for yourselves treasures
    on earth from day to day.
Give of your talent daily as through
    this life you go,
Everyone has been blessed with
    some kind, you know.

Sure others might have many more
    talents than you,
But that's no excuse for you not
    doing whatever you can do.
Just work with your talent religiously and
    tend it with loving care

And with a continuous expression of it
    others will become aware.

Don't bury your talent just because
    you have only one,
For if everyone felt this way, very
    little would ever be done.
Then, don't envy someone else's talents,
    just do what you can do.
God gave talents to them and
    yours He gave to you.

Then give of your time just as God
    gives it so freely to you.
Use it wisely to do for others
    whatever you can do.
Take the time to read your Bible, and
    bow down and pray
And give thanks to God for
    giving you this day.

Take time for the young, take
    time for the old,
Take time to invite sinners to
    come into the fold.
Give of your time to spread a
    little sunshine and joy.
Give a little time to direct the life
    of some girl or boy.

Give of your time to help some
    struggling brother along,
Give of your time to keep some
    youth from going wrong.
If you do these things, the world would

see Stewardship in action
And deep down within, you'll get a
    feeling of satisfaction.

All of us are stewards of something
    left within our care
And unless we give our very best,
    we are being unfair
To the God who giveth but also
    taketh away
And we'll have to give an account of
    our Stewardship one day.

Jesus left a guide, and He
    laid out a plan,
So there wouldn't be any excuse
    for one single man.
So stop being negative and
    go ahead and do it.
You won't be a failure, for God
    will see to it.

Be Grateful

Be grateful, things could be worse
    than they are.
Your life could be worse than
    it is by far,
You can see, that's a blessing
    many would love.
You can hear the thunder as it
    roars from above.
You can walk, you can talk,
    that should count a lot.
Be grateful every day for whatever
    it is you've got.

Be grateful, your situation isn't as
    bad as you think.
Just because you're down now, why
    that could change in a wink.
Don't give up because things don't
    always go your way,
For though life is uncertain, there'll
    probably be a better day.
Be grateful that you can think
    and love and give.
Just be grateful for the wonderful
    opportunity to live.

Assurance

Whether my days be long or short is naught to me;
As long as my life, dear God, has been pleasing to Thee.
Whether my earthly gain be great or small
Just doesn't really matter to me at all
As long as I keep the Lord on my side
And can in His love always peacefully abide.
I can make it through any kind of weather
Just my God and me always walking together.

Keep the Faith

When mountains seem insurmountable
and the valleys are unusually low,
When the pain inside you is growing and
there's no peace no matter where you go,
It's then you must turn your attention to
your Heavenly Father up above.
He sees and understands your problems and will
in time solve them with love.
When you have done all that you can do
in whatever the situation
And it seems that the end result is
only pain and frustration,
Don't throw your hands up and
wallow in self-pity and despair.
Just remember that the God of the
ages is in the background and He's aware.
He knows every thought even before
you have a chance to think it,

And He's certainly familiar with life's bitter
cup, for He Himself had to drink it.
He too was tempted of Satan when He
was both tired and weak,
But instead of yielding, God's divine
guidance He did seek
It doesn't matter how steep the mountain,
it always has a peak,
And it doesn't matter how far you've strayed,
God's divine guidance you too can seek.
He knows your problems and how
they can and will affect you
And if you diligently seek Him, He'll
in no way reject you.
He never promised that things in this life
would always be great,
But he did admonish us to trust in Him
and patiently wait
And in His own time, He'll straighten
everything out
And then you'll smile and wonder what
your worrying was all about.

Why Doubt?

Tell me, dear friend, why is thy
    heart all astir
And not at peace with God as
    in times past it were?
He hast never turned his back
    away from thee,

Nor hast He your loving Saviour
    ceased to be.
Hast thou not talked to Him lately
    or given a thought,
To all the wonderful miracles that
    He hast wrought?
From day to day all around and
    even including you,
Tell me, what more would thou have
    Him to do?
Did he not awaken you this wonderful
    morning so fair
After having kept you all night long
    in His loving care?
Were you not blessed to move and
    get out of bed,
Clothe yourself and see that your entire
    family was fed?
Did He not keep you from hurt or harm
    all the blessed day
As you did your work or just casually
    went your way?
Hast He not told you to cast all
    your cares to Him
And He would gladly help you to
    bear each of them?
Hast thou so quickly forgotten that
    dark day in Calvary
When he so freely gave His life for both
    you and me?
How then canst thy heart remain
    troubled and unsure?
Just keep the faith and He'll help you
    anything to endure.

How Will You React?

I

It's easy enough to smile when things
    are going fine
When there's shelter over your head and food
    on which to dine.
It's easy enough to be pleasant when things
    are going your way,
When prosperity is freely flowing and your
    life is happy and gay,
When your clothes are stylish and you're riding
    in a fine car
And everywhere you go someone recognizing
    who you are.

II

It's fine to go to church when nothing
    is going wrong
And mingle with the people and
    sing religious songs,
And greet your friends as before the
    church you leave
After the benediction has been by
    everyone received,
But what about the days that, without a
    doubt will come
When you'll encounter problems
    just like everyone?

III

How will you react when those troubles
    come your way?
Will you think about God's goodness
    to you and say
I'll still trust in Him whatever
    the outcome may be,
For this could very well be God's way
    of testing me,
To see if I would keep the faith even
    though times are rough.
I can't speak for you but, whatever my plight,
    His word is good enough.

Give Your Best

Do for the Master all you can each day.
Be sincere and humble as you watch and pray.
Give to a fellowman when you see him in need,
And on the word of God constantly feed.

Give Him the praise both day and night.
Love as Jesus loved and do what is right.
Try to bring sunshine into some dim life.
Do what you can to dispel hatred, trouble, and strife.

Pray without ceasing and always do your best.
Lift Him up and He's promised to do the rest.
Ask for His guidance in everything you do.
And always remember, the Lord is depending on you.

82

Share

Learn to share what God has
given to you,
For many of your blessings are needed
by others too.
Give a smile, that can oftentimes
be quite enough
To calm some weary soul with
troubles engulfed.
Give a kind word, sometimes that's
all that is needed,
To encourage someone who has
never succeeded.
Give a pat on the back of some
fellowman
Who is laden with the many problems
of this land.
Share your ideas with other
people who
Might not be able to think as
well as you.
Share your happy memories, others
need to know,
That life isn't all downhill and
without glow.

Guide Me

Dear God, guide me lest I stray
From the path of right in my own willful way.
For the best that I am or ever hope to be
Is naught, Dear God, in comparison to Thee.
For try as I will, I'm still but dust
And will cause You shame and betray Your trust
Unless You let me hold on to Your mighty hand
And on Your holy word, reverently stand.
For old Satan is mighty and has tricks to spare
And to let a Christian alone, he just wouldn't dare.
So Your guidance, Dear God, is my main concern
Lest I sink to the bottomless pit of the point of no return.

The Harvest

The harvest is truly great but the laborers are few.
Can't you see, Christian friends, what a job we have to do?
To gather the strayed souls back into the fold
And onto God's hand keep a firm and steadly hold.
Remember He's holding you responsible as well as He is
me,
For He's the Master Reaper and to eternal life holds the
key.
So don't get left out because your job here you've shirked.
Stay out there in the field and continue to do His work.
Then one day, we can reap a harvest far beyond compare,
When we enter into His presence and live with Him there,
In a wonderful place too great for human minds to
envision—
The choice is ours, so let's make the right decision.

Accept Whatever Comes

There are times in life when I feel
     like a milliionaire,
And breeze along easily without a
     worry or care.
Some days I am just as happy as a king
     upon his throne
Whether I'm mingling with a crowd or
     meditating with God alone.

There are times in life when nothing
     seems to go right,
Even though I'm careful and work
     with all my might
Trying to do what's right as I
     go from day to day
And inject a little happiness and
     sunshine along the way.

But regardless of disappointments and some
     days filled with cheer,
I know there's a reason for all of these
     things that appear.
The answer to none of these things
     do I ever try to seek.
I just pray to always remain patient,
     humble and meek,
For I realize that some of it must be a
     part of God's plan
And I'll just accept whatever comes
     and do the best I can.

The Clock of Life

As the clock of time slowly ticks
each day,
And each individual goes quietly
his way,
Each time the pendulum of the big
clock swings,
It brings about changes in so
many things.
It changes us from innocent children to
adults so bold.
It also causes many of life's mysteries
to us, unfold.
It changes us from teenagers so happy
and carefree,
To the men and women we were
destined to be.
We often lose simple honesty and
childlike trust
And become wayfarers of this
world's lust.
It changes some young boys to
men overnight,
And forces them to make decisions on
wrong and right.
It turns many beautiful girls into
women of the night
And causes them to oftentimes
lose sight
Of the Christian home training of
Mom and Dad
Whom they find too late, many times, were the best
friends they had.

It turns sharp minds into minds
that are senile,
Minds that, for years, could others
so easily beguile.
The clock of time can bring both
joy and pain,
Before our bodies are in the
cold earth lain.
So as life's clock ticks slowly
day by day,
It behooves us to watch, friends,
as well as pray,
For we can't turn back the hands or
alter the time.
Even if another chance we had, our lives
would not be sublime.

Hospitality

H is for the happiness that we
feel today.

O is for the opportunities you opened
along the way.

S is for the sweetness always reflected
in your face.

P is for the patience you've shown the
whole human race.

I is for the illiteracy you tried so
hard to erase.

T is for the troubles that were on your
shoulders placed.

A is for the adoration that we all
have for you.

L is for the love that you've shared
with us too.

I is for the great image you have
always reflected.

T is for the timely move we made when
you were elected.

Y is for yourself of which you've given
your all.

Put them all together and they
spell hospitality,

In touch with both your fellowman
and reality.

A Christian's Garden

If you would like a good Christian
    garden successfully to grow,
Listen intently, for there are some
    things you'll need to know.
A Christian garden you won't
    be able to grow
In soil poisoned by ungodly,
    sinful things, you know.
First tap the vast resources of Heaven
    by earnestly talking to God,
And if you're sincere, He'll respond
    by preparing the sod.
Plant something worthwhile daily through
    kind words and deeds,
Then stand back and watch how God
    will multiply those seeds.
Think of the farmer—he dares not to sit
    and hold his hands
And then at harvest time expect
    great yield of the land.
Then how much more diligent we
Christians must plan
In sowing only good seeds for
    the good of man.
There are some seeds a Christian
    garden must possess
That is, if you want to make sure
    it will be a success.
Begin with the seed of faith, for without it
    the harvest can't grow.
Then add a row of humility to help
    as you face the foe.

Plant a long row of hope, for it
    will keep you going along,
And reflect a ray of sunshine when
    things are going wrong.
Please don't forget the seed of patience as
    you plant this crop,
For it will help you and encourage
    others not to stop.
Leave some space for understanding and
    don't be so quick to complain,
For you must remember a crop needs
    sunshine as well as rain.
Don't forget joy, for it will help
    to make others glad.
After all, at times, your heart has
    been burdened and sad.
Plant several rows of forgiveness
    for every sister and brother,
For did not Jesus say that we
    must forgive one another?
Then last but most important,
    add several rows of love.
I mean the real true kind that's
    transmitted from above.
Tend these seeds carefully and chop away
    all weeds of doubt,
For when God sent His son, not one
    of us was left out.
Then at harvest time only Godly
    things your crop will yield
And all because you planted all good
    seeds in life's field.

Remember Your Promise

Fields are white and harvest waiting,
the Master still calls today,
So stand not idly here and
continue to procrastinate.
Go out there in the fields and work
day in and out.
Just do your share and you'll be
paid without a doubt.
It's mighty easy to complain I'm
so tired and weak,
But the Master's blessings, daily, we
continue to seek.
Look not for others to help you
do your share,
For they too have some heavy
burdens to bear.
The gathering of the harvest depends
entirely upon you.
After all, this is what you promised
the Lord you would do.
You did not say, Lord, I'll work
if I have the time
And He did not promise that you'd
have a life sublime.
So just hang on in there and do
what you promised to do,
And without a doubt, I know I'm right,
my God will see you through.

Lest I Forget

I

Lest I forget, dear God, from whence I came,
Let me not so quickly others to blame,
For the wrong things they might do and say
Because many times, in life, God's will I did not obey.
I have not always walked in the path of right
And been to mankind a guiding light.
I have not always striven to keep my cool
And follow each day of my life the golden rule.
Let me not forget that I've been wrongly accused,
And it left me broken-hearted and confused.
So help me to sympathize with each and every one
And keep faith in humanity till this life is done.

II

Lest I forget the hard struggle by my Mom and Dad,
To give us so many opportunities they never had.
Help me to do for them all I can along the way
To make life both easy and happy for them each day.
Let me not forget when my cupboards were bare
So keep me sympathetic toward those less fortunate
than I,

And help me to do many good deeds before I die.
Let me never forget those who helped me along,
Even though, from this life, some of them are gone.
Let me not fail them by betraying their trust,
Even though temptations upon me many times are thrust.
Just help me to keep this thought forever before me,
Lest I forget from whence I came and fail daily to give
thanks to Thee.

Negativism in the Church

"Why is there so much negativism in the church?" I was
asked one day,
And I pondered a long time trying to think of what to say.
Then I said to myself, "I think I'll begin with me
And try to analyze just what the trouble might be."
Well, here's the answer that I finally came upon
As I sat deep in thought in a room all alone.
When I accepted Christ, I was really ambitious and filled
with ideas
To share this great feeling with everyone, and especially
with my peers.
I was all charged up, ready and anxious to do
All the things the Bible had said Christ wanted me to.
But my spirit was crushed right from the start,
By persons who'd been in church for years with sin-sick
hearts.
Instead of placing their arms around me and showing me
the way,
They made snide remarks and criticized whatever I had
to say.
But with the wonderful guidance of my mother's hand,
As I became older and studied my Bible, I began to
understand
That Christ must not have meant to them what He means
to me,
As I had been taught from childhood around my mother's
knee.
If I'd suggest an idea and say let's do that or this,
The opportunity to knock at someone would never miss.
Then there were some ministers for whom I had great
respect
Who, to some extent, went to great length to aid and abet
Other members who, for no apparent reason, were out to

get me,
Simply because I would dare to do things as they needed
to be.
So somewhere along the line as the years rolled on,
I began to become suspicious of practically everyone.
When I was shown a negative attitude, I began to throw
one back,
And at times, my participation in things became pretty
slack.
I began to lose faith in both women and men,
And it pulled me away from the closeness to Christ where
I'd been.
It bothered me so much 'til I couldn't sleep at night
And going on within my inner being was an awful flight.
Not only couldn't I sleep at night, but I was restless during
the day,
So I began to search myself and sincerely began to pray.
My prayer wasn't by any means a selfish one,
I prayed also for my oppressors and to let God's will be
done.
And when I prayed this prayer—not my will but Your will,
He immediately restored my faith and spiritual cup
refilled.
Soon I began to say, yes, I'll do my best, but never no,
For He'd given his assurance that always with me He
would go.
So maybe that's why so much negativism is in the church.
You need sincerely and thoroughly your own soul to
search,
To see if you are guilty in any way of causing another
pain
Or if you are into this thing for your own personal gain.
See if you've wounded the spirit of even a child today
By being negative to them in what you had to say.

So many things are happening to cause negativism in our
church today,
But make sure you're not guilty, for if you are, you too
someday will pay.

A Glimpse of Heaven

Have you ever watched a little child at play,
So sweet, so innocent, happy and gay,
So pleased with the world and everything within,
Completely unaware of ugliness, vice, and sin,
Finding wonder in loving everyone and everything,
From the worm that crawls to the bird that sings.
The wild flowers that spring up around the door,
The tiny bug that crawls on the floor.
Loving the tenderness in a mother's sweet smile,
Building a castle in the park's sand pile.
A glimpse of Heaven can be seen in that child,
So meek, so precious, so humble and mild.

A Gift from God

A child is a gift from God, so
    we should be careful to

Do everything in our power that
    we can possibly do

To see that it is nourished and
    handled with care and love,

For we'll have to answer for our role
    in that child's life to God above.

Christians Working for the
Up-building of God's Kingdom

Christians, you have a mighty big job to do,
And your heavenly Father is depending on you
To carry His message throughout the world today
By the work that you do and the things you say.
You can't be saved by works—indeed you cannot,
But working daily for Him will help a lot
To reach that lost soul who is out in the cold
And the true meaning of Christ to him unfold.
Or give hope to the downtrodden who are in despair
And prove to them there's a God who really does care.
Work to bring about peace rather than confusion and
strife,
Thereby helping to insure for yourself eternal life.
Work to give happiness where there is sorrow and pain,
You have nothing to lose and everything to gain.
God needs your eyes to see suffering in the world today
And help some weary travelers along life's way.
He needs your ears to hear their cries of pain
While through riotous living, good times they try to feign.
He needs your hands to administer to their many needs
And serve them daily by doing good deeds.
He needs your feet to go oft times into unpleasant places
Where you won't be welcomed by many creeds and races.
He needs your heart with compassion to fill
So that you'll always be willing to do His will.
He needs your tongue to tell of His love so true,
And spread the good news that Christ died for you.
But Christians, before you can begin this task today,
You must first humble yourselves and sincerely pray,
For the up-building of His kingdom begins with us

And doesn't call for outside show and fuss,
Merely a lot of hard work and true dedication,
Humbleness of heart and sincere consecration.
If we equip ourselves with these tools of love,
God's kingdom here will be likened to the one above.

My Silent Partner

As I ascend this steep highway of life
Mid turmoil, pressure, envy, and strife,
I've been asked by friends time and time again
Just how I'm able to withstand the wiles of man;
The open stares, sarcastic remarks, and scornful looks,
The shameless schemes and snares of guileful crooks,
The petty things by jealous comrades often said,
The many roadblocks set up to keep me from getting
ahead,
The many digs to try and make me retreat
Into a shell of self-pity and make me accept defeat.

Well, it took me a long time to reach this state.
It took lots of patience and accepting the fate
That seemingly was destined to be mine
And looking constantly ahead and seldom behind.
And I learned, the hard way, many years ago
To never give in to the schemes of a foe,
Or agree with a friend when I know he is wrong,
And always to keep deep in my heart a song.
Then above all, the thing that most folks don't know
Is, that there's a silent partner walking with me wherever
I go.

What Is Your Purpose in Life?

I

When life seems dull and nothing to do you can find,
When everything goes wrong and you have no peace of
mind,
When the days become boring and all the nights long,
You'd better stop and take a look to see just what is wrong.
And find what your purpose in life is, my friend,
Then start immediately to work toward that end.

II

For life is too important and troubles far too great
To trudge carelessly along at a nonchalant pace.
A life without purpose simply can't continue to stand,
In a world today filled to the brim with demands.
So get busy, take inventory of yourself and find
Your purpose for living and get some peace of mind.

III

It might not be that you'll take the world by storm,
But at least you'll be happy to know where you are going.
It might be a matter of steadily moving along the road
And pausing to help a faltering brother carry his load.
Or a pat on the back of a friend when things are going
rough
Or a few words of comfort might oft times be enough
To calm a man's fears and to his life real meaning give,
For the life without a purpose has truly failed to live.

Christians in the Mainstream with Christ

I

In the mainstream with Christ is no easy place to stay,
For you'll be tried and tempted by Satan every day.
You'll be tested by enemies, friends, and loved ones too,
And the whole world will be keeping an eye on you.
Innocent words you speak will be twisted without shame,
And things, for which you're not guilty, you'll bear the
blame.
You'll be talked about shamefully and often times
misunderstood,
Even after you've done your best and tried to work for
good.
It means trudging steadily along when the road is long;
It means loving humanity, even though they've done you
wrong.
It means forcing a smile when you really want to frown;
It means going that extra mile even though you've been
let down.

II

But if you stay in the mainstream with Christ in spite of
these things,
Your hopes and aspirations will no longer just be dreams.
You'll be able to look the whole world squarely in the face
And have love in your heart for the whole human race.
You'll be able to say "I can" when you can't see your way.
You'll be able to wait with patience come what may.
You'll be able to give hope to the hopeless and peace to
troubled minds,

99

And lead them to Christ that He may make their lives
sublime.
It means letting Him guide you as out into the world
you're sent,
And walking in the rugged path where Christ often went.
For Christians—to be in the mainstream with Christ
Simply means letting Him take full control of your life.

So We Go Singing Onward

Mid turmoil, troubles and strife,
And all unpleasantries that make up life,
Mid sad days and days filled with love,
Through happy days and blue skies above,
You know not sometimes just what to do
Though there's an all-seeing eye watching you,
So we go singing onward.

God has a plan for both you and me,
Though just what sometimes we cannot see,
Until we dedicate ourselves and watch and pray
And sincerely seek His guidance day by day,
And make His will our command
And be guided daily by His hand,
While we go singing onward.

We sing His praises day in and day out
As we do our work and walk about.
We raise hymns with voices sweet and clear,
And sing them loudly with hearts sincere.
Their true meanings to each of us unfold
As we hear the stories so sweetly retold.
And we go singing onward.

A Bridge Builder

(For a Retiring Teacher)

You have built many intellectual bridges
    that span the times,
Be helping to develop hundreds
    and hundreds of minds.
Back when you started you had
    great parental cooperation
And looked forward to going to work
    with great anticipation.
The salary was low and the
    record-keeping immense
With those complicated registers that
    didn't make much sense.
You went to school whether there
    was rain, snow or sleet,
For you knew there were books your children
    had to complete.
You've, no doubt, taught in situations
    far from ideal
But tried to make students understand that life
    out there is real.
You've instilled worthwhile values in
    more children than you know
That are proving to be prosperous as through
    this life they go;
The right to make decisions regarding punishment
    was left to your discretion
And many who are successful today, you
    started in the right direction.
In spite of all the changes, you just
    hung in there and taught,

For you knew that successful students could
    only by good teaching be wrought.
You've seen so many programs from
    the top eagerly sent
And oftentimes soon after receiving them
    they quickly went.
You knew from experience what it took
    to get the job done
And you didn't try to convince them
    that all learning was fun.
You built bridges of kindness, aspirations,
    love, good manners, honesty and trust,
For you knew if they were to succeed in life,
    all of these virtues were a must.
And now the time has come for you
    to bid each of us adieu,
But your great work has gone down in history
    and we want you to know that we'll miss you.

It's Later than You Think

Be careful how you walk today
Be careful how you speak today
Be sure you do some good today,
For it's later than you think.

Befriend a fellowman today
Commune with God today
Study God's holy word today,
It's later than you think.

Pass along a smile today
Slow down, take time out today
Enjoy the beauty of nature today,
For it's later than you think.

Help to bear someone's burdens today
Visit the sick and shut-in today
Share what you're blessed with today,
It's later than you think.

Bridle that vicious tongue today
Say something good about someone today
Let someone know you care today,
For it's later than you think.

A Virtuous Woman

A virtuous woman in times like these,
To remain that way, must stay on her knees,
And when life's storms come as they're sure to do,
Just remember it's not just happening to you.
You just know about yours and it seems rough,
But for many others, too, the going is tough.
Keep in mind you were not promised a life of ease
And from troubles you would get a release.
For if you were not tested, how would it be known
Just how strong your life in Christ has grown.
If there was no bitter, how would you enjoy the sweet
And look forward someday your Savior's face to meet?

A virtuous woman must be sincere, humble, and kind,
And keep God's work uppermost in her mind.
This does not mean to ignore the things of this life.
After all, you took a vow to be a devoted wife,
And relieve the vast suffering of all mankind
And do whatever else your hands can find
To bring people to Christ and hope to them give
So they can really and truly begin to live.
Many a Christian woman has already stood the test,
Held on firmly to God's hand and did her best,
In spite of the turmoil and troubles of this life,
She has continued to be a virtuous wife.

Somebody Cares

It's so good to know that there is someone to care
And your hopes and joys as well as burdens share,
Who won't rejoice when things in your life go wrong,
But will console you and tell you it won't be long
Till things get better and your load'll get lighter,
The long nights shorter and the dark days brighter.

It's a wonderful feeling to know you're never alone,
Even when all of your earthly friends are gone,
The ones that you helped when they were down
Who only glance your way, ignore you and frown.
When even your loved ones begin to act queer,
And try to avoid you whenever you are near.
There's a blessed assurance just in knowing
That someday with Christ I'll be going
To that eternal home that He has prepared
And with other saints it will be joyfully shared.
Yes, I'm grateful that Christ will always care,
And of His presence I'm constantly aware.

I Wonder

If the world wasn't filled with misery and strife,
I wonder what we would accomplish in this life.
If all roads were smooth and cares were nil,
I wonder would we ever think of Calvary's hill.

If there were no troubles to press us down,
If there was always laughter and never a frown,
If worry was deceased and cares unknown,
I wonder would there have to be an eternal throne.

Then I wonder if there was more love and a lot less hate,
And more good deeds and less talk about the pearly gates,
Wouldn't life really be a bit more worth living,
With souls more sincere and hearts more forgiving.

I wonder will the time ever come when men of all races,
Will work together harmoniously regardless of the color
of their faces.
If this time does come for all of use to see,
Then we won't have to wonder where we'll spend eternity.

Why

"I wonder why Jesus would love us so,"
Said a little girl to her mother long ago.
"You said that He died for you and me.
Why would He do this, I just can't see.
We are very mean and do not obey,
And yet, He still loves us you say.
Why would He choose to die on the cross
So even the bad folk would not be lost?
They didn't love Him—I know He could see
Or they wouldn't have nailed Him to the tree.
His own followers didn't try to save Him,
And yet on the cross He still forgave them.
And, Mother, you say He still loves us today,
The rich in their mansions and the children at play.
We still do things that would not please Him.
I hate to think of how much it must grieve Him."

"Listen, darling, while I try to explain
Just why Jesus chose to bear this pain.
No—none of us are worthy of His precious love,
Nor the agony He suffered before going above.
He knew this, yet in spite of it all,
He did not want to see us fall
Into the hands of Satan who is anxious to see
What evil people he can make of you and me.
"You see, the love He has is greater than ours.
It extends to every animal, plant, and flower,
The rich, the poor, the happy, the sad,
The homely, the pretty, the good and the bad.
Never before a precious gift so full of love,
Neither on the lowly earth nor in Heaven above
Had ever been given in the history of man.
So darling, maybe that's why it's so hard to understand.
Anyway we know it all had to be a part of God's plan."

My Prayer

Dear God, guide my hands that they might do
The things in life that You have equipped them to.
Guide my feet that they might always go
In the places You wish midst friend or foe.
Guide my eyes so that they might see
The kind of person You would have me be.
Guide my mind to have a goal in view,
One worthwhile and in every way depicting You.
Guide my ears so that they might hear
And relieve some of the suffering, pain, and tears
In others that from day to day I meet
That they might hold on in the face of defeat.
Then, dear God, guide my lips so that they might tell
Of your wonderful love which will all our troubles quell.

Count the Cost

Before you jump in and make
that hasty decision,
Think of how it will affect others
or if it's an imposition
On someone else and might
cause them pain
And ask yourself, "Now what do
I hope to gain?"
Before you repeat that gossip
you just heard,
Think, it might not be true
not a single word.
Remember how you felt when others
gossiped about you,
Especially when you knew that

it was not true.
So before some valued friendship
is lost,
Take just a minute to count
the cost.

A Sinner Repents

A Christian and a sinner stood talking one day,
And the conversation they had went this way.
Said the sinner to the Christian with a cunning little grin.
"Tell me, good brother, just where have you been?
To the church on the hill to give the preacher your money
And listen to all that jive about the land of milk and
honey—
About the angelic choir and all that Heavenly Host.
I'm sure that's all he knows to tell you folks
And preach about this awful world—how it's filled with
sin.
While all the time he keeps raking all that money in—
Why don't you wake up, friend, and really get wise,
'Cause once you're dead, man, you sure ain't gonna rise.
Now just look at me; you can see I'm doing just fine.
I've got money in my pockets and can wine and dine
In the very finest restaurants that can be found.
And, I own quite a bit of property in this little town;
And another thing, people look up to me wherever I go
'Cause they know I've got power and plenty of dough.
So tell me, friend, who is more prosperous and getting
the best deal?
Who's living in a dream world and whose life is real?"

The Christian stood solemnly thinking of all the man said,
But soon gave him a long, hard look and sadly shook his
head.
"I wish, good brother, that I could make you see
What you're missing, and how sweet your life in Christ
can be.
Those material things that you speak of are all right to
possess,
But be honest with yourself—do they bring you real
happiness?
I mean the kind of happiness that fills your very heart
Because in helping a faltering brother, you know you had
a part.
Do you know the joy of giving when you really have
nothing to give
But a few words of encouragement to someone who doesn't
want to live?
Have you experienced the peace of mind you get from
helping someone
And doing all the good deeds you can before another
setting sun?
Have you witnessed the fellowship of that little
congregation on the hill?
Have you seen them bow at the altar to have their
spiritual cups refilled?
Would that you could hear the choir softly singing
'Amazing Grace,'
And see tears of happiness flowing proudly down the
Christians' face.
Have you seen the children's anxious eyes as they hear
Bible stories of old
And see their faces light up as the real meaning to them
unfolds?
Would that you hear the preacher pouring out the

message from above
And see the old soldiers craving to share their knowledge
of Jesus' love,
And then the youth, so full of life, come eager to learn
all that they can
About that solitary life of God's greatest gift to man.
I could just go on and on until death temporarily closes
my lips
And still from your soul that ugly sin I could not rip,
For until you are willing to open your heart and let God
come in,
You'll continue to live a useless life and die a death of
immortal sin."
The sinner lifted his head, which had long since been
bowed down,
Then grasping the Christian's hands, fell to his knees on
the ground.
"Dear brother, while standing here all this time listening
to you," said he,
"God has revealed so many things I'd never thought of
through thee.
The things I bragged about now seem so unimportant and
needless,
That it's hard to believe that my life has been so sinful
and heedless.
I've taken his blessings for granted with a selfish and
arrogant air,
And for all the things He's given me, I've never even
offered a prayer.
I've trampled on so many people to obtain what I've got,
And the things of this world have always meant a lot.
I'd never thought of others who are less fortunate than I;
I'd never even thought of the fact that someday I'd have
to lay down and die.

I've given my children everything they needed except
guidance and love.
I only hope and trust that there is someone somewhere
up above
Who will help me to redirect my path and dedicate my
life to Him
Then touch my wife and children and help me to be an
example for them.
And help me to restore fourfold to everyone that I have
cheated
And continue in Thy love so that none of these awful sins
will be repeated.
So thank you Lord, for opening my eyes through this
Christian man,
For it has been through his witness that I've accepted
Heaven's great plan."

I Know He's There

Even though I can't see God, I
know He's there
In the grass, the trees, the flowers
and everywhere.
I can feel His presence when in the
bed I lie
Or watch a beautiful sunset in the
western sky.
I can see Him in a little child, so humble
innocent and sweet,
Or in the vast fields of lovely
flowing wheat.

I can hear Him in the birds that sing
and soar so high,
And feel Him in the gentle rain blowing
from the sky.
I can see Him in the beautiful flowers
blooming so fair,
As the sweet smelling fragrance floats
through the air.
I can see Him in the garden as the
vegetables begin to grow,
For the secret they have with nature
man doesn't know.
I can see Him in the hearts of so
many of my fellowmen,
And feel Him moving on the altar of my heart
every now and then.
I can see Him in my dear mother
and my father too
And in the lakes, the rivers, ponds
and oceans blue.
I can see Him in the mountains so
very big and tall,
The plains, the plateaus, the hills, the
snow that falls.
If you'll just take a good look
all around you,
You'll see Him in others and they'll see
Him in you too.

Death

Death is an intruder who is afraid of no man.
He stalks in wait and strikes wherever he can.
He's feared and dreaded by both young and old,
And his mysteries, to us, seem never to quite unfold.
We know he's coming to all of our doors one day;
Yet, when he arrives, we can't find words to say.
For even though we're expecting him, we're never quite ready,
And it leaves tears in our eyes and our voices unsteady.
So heartbroken, and sorry and burdened we are,
Till our grief casts a shadow on Calvary's hill afar.
A shadow so huge that through it we fail to see
The great sacrifice Jesus made for you and me.
He conquered death in the grave many years ago
So that Christians would not consider death to be a foe.
If you can't think of that, just try to remember this,
That death is a short interval before a life of bliss.

Just Trust in God

Put all your trust in my God above,
And never either question or doubt His love.
Live for Him in all you attempt to do or say
And walk as He'd have you walk from day to day.
Keep your hand in His and never let go,
For He'll do just what He said, this I know.
Treat everyone right whatever you do
And have the assurance that He'll watch over you.
When the storms of life come, as they're sure to do,

Hang in there and let Him know He can count on you.
Be patient, forgiving, humble, honest and true.
Give your best to Him, for He'll do the same for you.
Pray without ceasing and do whatever you can
To give ease and comfort to a fellowman.
Read your Bible and feast on it in your heart,
And never ever from righteousness stray or depart.

Life's Crossroads

I came to life's crossroads one day many years ago.
I stood there and pondered on which way I should go.
One mind said go that while the other said go this
And a good time in this life you can't miss.
I chose the one that promised good times and fun,
Not really realizing just what I had done.
I went on down the road for many, many years,
Until it caused me grief and made me shed briny tears.
It almost destroyed my health and affected my mind
Until inner peace I thought I'd never again find.
And then one day I heard a still small voice
Saying, "Don't give up, you can still make the right choice.
Just turn around now and take the other road.
God is standing there waiting to help you carry your load.
He's watched you sin, frolic, and carelessly roam,
But He has outstretched arms just to welcome you home.
The choice was yours and the wrong one you made,
But when Christ went to Calvary, that debt was paid."
So I got on the right road beginning that day,
And ever since, I've been on the King's highway.

My Rendezvous with God

In the wee hours of the morning when I can't seem to sleep,
I climb quietly out of bed and on my knees reverently creep
To commune with God and thank Him for His invitation,
To meet Him there, just a small but holy congregation.
Everyone in the house has long since been asleep
And the night is so peaceful, dark, calm and deep.
I call on His name and He doesn't fail to respond,
For He remembers that many years ago we made a bond
That He'd come to my rescue and hear my plea,
If I would do His bidding and His servant be.
And regardless of the problem, He has never failed me,
It gives me peace of mind to the highest degree.
He assures me that life is really worth living,
With its twists and turns and souls unforgiving.
He gives me courage and hope to face the coming day,
So that I'm stronger to face the things that come my way.
Then I say "Thank you, Lord, for letting me lie here
awake,
Otherwise, this communion with Thee, I could not
partake."
Then I ease back into bed so happy and content,
For my rendezvous with God was time well spent.

⅄ *What Keeps Me Going*

What keeps me going when the chips are down?
What makes me keep my head up and stand my ground
When evil surrounds me like a blanket of stagnant air
And comfort and peace I can't seem to find anywhere?
What pushes me on when all my strength seems gone
When I feel unloved, comfortless, and so all alone?
What seals my lips when my soul is in despair
Crying from life's knocks of which I've had my share?
What keeps me plodding along in the face of defeat
Even though it seems useless and my head says retreat—
When my heart, with sorrow, is filled to the brim
And the long road ahead seems so lonely and dim
Well, I'll tell you what keeps me going in spite of these things,
Not talk of walking golden streets and wearing angel wings.
It's the relief I see in the face of a fellowman
When I go to his rescue and lend a helping hand.
It's the piece of bread that I share with a hungry soul
And going that extra mile to help someone attain his goal.
It's the gratitude seen in the face of a boy gone wrong
When I've led him to Christ and in his heart left a song;
It's the humble look on the face of a girl fallen from grace
Who has learned her lesson and is ready to take her place
In society and help others to profit by her mistake—
It's talking with the Master when no one else in the house
is awake.

Father, Forgive Me

Father, forgive me if I have sinned today
In failing to, your pleading voice obey.
Help me to be determined Thy will to do,
To walk in Your footsteps and act like You.
To be ever conscious of blessings bestowed on me,
Blessings that are both abundant and free.

Forgive me, Lord, when I sometimes complain,
Or become selfish, haughty, and vain.
When I frown when I should give a smile
To a fellowman who is down for a while.
Help me to always think before I speak
And offer comfort to the downtrodden and weak.
Help me to forgive others who've done wrong to me,
And show to them what being Christlike can be.
Help me to always let my little light shine
To guide others into the paths that are Thine.
Help me to love with a love that is true,
Regardless of what others may say or do.
Help me to bridle my tongue, lest it defile someone,
And work for Thee till this life is done.

God's Masterpiece

The world is a breathtaking portrait painted by God,
With its towering mountains and beautiful green sod,
With its billowy trees and blooming flowers.
And all of this, at no cost, is ours
To enjoy and admire as we go carelessly along
Not even giving a thought about to whom they belong.

The waters of splendor, the bountiful hills and plains,
The beautiful golden sunsets and purifying rains,
The fields of green clover so divinely planted,
The heavenly bodies that we all take for granted,
The snowy peaks and the lovely rainbow rare,
The flowers wild needing not our care,
The birds soaring high wondering not their fate;
The scene is beautiful and the Painter how great!

No Peace

When my back's against the wall and I
don't know which way to turn,
When everything's going wrong and for
peace of mind I yearn,
When troubles seem to come in battalions
and not a friend in sight,
When on a tear-stained pillow I've
tossed throughout the night,
When I've exhausted every measure
in this finite mind,
And answers to my problems I
still cannot find,
It is then that I turn to Jesus and He
comes to my rescue
And sets things aright, for He knows
exactly what to do
To relieve the suffering and give
ease to my pain
And reassure me that He loves me
over and over again.

Don't Quit

When things in life go wrong, as they're sure to do,
And everyone around seems to be prospering but you;
When the days seem long and the nights are dreary
And life's constant struggle has you tired and weary;
when friends deceive you and loved ones don't care a bit,
Just pray a little harder, but don't you dare quit.

When everything goes wrong though you've done your all,
And the load you're carrying is about to make you fall;
When you think you've had it and must stop to rest,
Just remember, stopping never helped anyone pass the
test.
When the sunshine and blue skies seem so far away,
When you've exhausted all measures and have nothing
to say,
Turn to Jesus, He knows that you have done your bit,
Then pray a little harder, but don't ever quit.

When for no apparent reason people turn their backs,
When the cooperation you once had becomes very slack;
When friends' hostility and indifference cause you pain,
And these attitudes toward you you cannot explain;
Just remember, you're not the first and won't be the last,
For it has happened to others, greater than you, in the
past.
Just keep on pushing and continuing to do your bit,
And pray a little more—but don't ever quit.

I Prayed for You Today

Katherine, I said a prayer for both you and Allen today,
I asked the Lord to protect and guide you along the way.
I asked Him to help you to humbly accept His will
And to let you know that He loves both of you still.
I prayed that He would give you the wisdom to know
That He will be with you no matter where you go.
I know it's not easy to lose someone close to you,
I know and I understand because I've been there too.
A special favor of God I sincerely did ask
That He would let you go about your daily tasks—
And give you the endurance to bear the pain,
For only time and time alone will help it to wane.
Lewis has crossed the chasm that we too one day will
cross
Though his leaving, for many, is such a terrible loss.
Cry if you must, but remember and cherish all of the time
That his presence with you made your lives sublime.
His suffering is now over and Lewis wants you to be brave
And trust in Almighty God so that He your souls will save.

An If for Christians

If you knew that life would end with the close of day
And that your feet would never again pass this way,
If you knew for sure that with today's setting sun
Your assignment here on this earth would be done,
If you knew that your lips would never again speak
And no other chance you'd have God's forgiveness to seek,
If you knew that regardless of how hard you tried
Another chance to improve yourself would be denied,
Would you have done the same things you did today,
And moved carelessly about in your usual way?
Or would you have tried just a little harder to do
The things that Christ would have wanted you to?
Would you have passed by that beggar on the street
As you walked into that exclusive restaurant to eat?
Would you have been a little more patient with your
mother,
Or ignored the simple favor that was asked by a brother?
Would you have taken time out to visit the sick?
And would that snide remark have been made so quick?
Or would you have been nicer to everyone you met
And did all the good deeds you could before the sun was
set?
So if you are given another chance to undo the wrongs
you've done,
Work hard each day for good, till life's battle is fought
and the victory won.

A Teacher's Prayer

Dear God, please never ever let
me dare
To neglect the children left daily in
my care,
Or crush their spirits, simple though
they be,
For to their future, I might hold
the key.
May I never let them down when they
need my aid
Or shrink, when on my shoulders their problems
are laid.

Dear God, give me the wisdom
to be
A teacher with endurance like
unto Thee,
To keep on striving through
words and deeds,
To find solutions to their problems and
supply their needs,
To open worthwhile avenues in
their young lives
That they might on life's right
road decide.
Amen

A Great Experience

Working with multi-ethnic children has been an
experience for me,
For the vast differences in them, I haven't been able to see.
Certainly, some prove to be more aggressive than others
are,
But very few have outdistanced the group by far.
Their concern for one another is truly real
And they care, for the most part, how others might feel.
They accept each other just by face value alone,
And get along fine, unless influenced by someone grown
Who is prejudiced and hopes to impede the great progress
Made through the years, for fear their powers will be less.
They express in so many little ways their love for me,
For I sincerely feel that each of them can see
How much I love them and give each day my best
To the smart ones, the slow ones, and all the rest.
One minute they're happy, the next they are mad,
But seldom do they do things that are really bad.
They pair off, not by race, but as friend to friend
And will go their limit, each other to defend.
Each little heart is as pure as the falling show,
With each little face many times all aglow
When they find out that everything the teacher doesn't
know,
And that they, to her, some information can bestow.
They all reflect happiness, sadness, wonder and concern,
But the most important thing is, each of them can learn.

Peace Within

I

When daylight is passed and shades of night softly appear,
I like to lie down and look back over a day of cheer.
Not cheer in the sense of good times and fun,
But joy in knowing that I have helped someone.
Maybe it was just a kind word or a very small deed
That helped someone who was sorely in need
Of the comfort I could give or the spirit I could brighten,
The smile I could bring or the load I could lighten.

II

When daylight is passed and shades of night softly appear,
I don't want to lie there restless because of fear.
Fear that I've missed my chance to serve mankind,
For if I did, this chance I might never again find.
Fear that I might have caused someone to go astray
To walk unheedingly in his own willful way.
Or failed to do something that would have helped
someone,
Something that could very easily have been done.
Fear that the shadows of life are approaching and find me
Unprepared to meet my Maker and with Him spend
eternity.

Check Your Life

Life is filled with disappointments, but it has its pleasures
too.
It all depends on your attitude and how you let things
get to you.
You can go through life complacent, unhappy, disgruntled
and unkind,
Or you can be calm, refreshing and exuberant, with inner
peace of mind.
You can radiate love and your life will be filled with joy,
Like a child on Christmas morn with a brand new toy,
Or you can reflect dissatisfication with everything and
everyone
And cause all the unhappiness you can before each day
is done.
You can try and drag others down as through this life
you go,
And make no worthwhile contributions in this world
below.
But remember, you reap what you sow, this is a proven fact,
So be careful of what you say and watch how you act.
For even though you might not realize it, someone is
watching you,
And they will act as you act and do as they see you do.
So think about this and let your life be one above reproof.
Don't walk around being critical, selfish and aloof.
Live each day as though you knew that it would be your
last,
Then you'll have no regrets about moving on when this
life is past.

A Job Transition

Now that this day has finally come
    I'm filled with emotion,
And it's all because of you—your
    wonderful love and devotion.
I've worked closely with many of you
    down through the years,
And we've shared many joys through
    blood, sweat, and tears.
For many years now, I've looked
    forward to this day
And now that it's here, I'm lost
    for words to say.
But as I look back on the many
    lives I've tried to touch,
I realize that, to me, each one
    has meant so very much.
I've tried to give the very best
    that I could possibly give
To help each child to realize that
    he has a right to live
And function in society the very
    best that he can,
For this is a God-given right
    to every single man.
I've tried to leave a few footprints
    as long the way I've trod.
I've tried to instill love for
    fellowmen and faith in God.
Even though I'm retiring, my thoughts
    will be with you,
And I'll be pulling for you and
    praying for you too,

That God will give the wisdom and
        the courage that you need
To reassure each child that in
        life he really can succeed.
I'm passing the torch along and
        a challenge here tonight
As others before me did that I would
        hold high the light
So some lost child might be able
        to find his way
And carry on his/her life's work
        in a special way.
I have no plans for going home to a
        comfortable rocking chair,
But this will be an opportunity to
        show others that I care,
By volunteering my services to the
        sick, the troubled and weak
And will open many avenues that I've
        long wanted to seek.
I thank God for so many wonderful
        friends like each of you here,
Who've come from far and near to celebrate
        and give me words of cheer.
You being here tonight means more to me
        than words could ever express,
And has brought joy to the depths of
        my heart and true happiness.
If you ever, ever really need me,
        please don't hesitate to call,
For I truly love and appreciate your
        kindness one and all.

Mary's Grief

I can imagine how burdened Mary
felt that day
When she watched them carry
her son away.
She stood there with her heart both
heavy and sad,
For this was the greatest sorrow she
had ever had,
Understanding His mission and certainly
knowing His fate,
But she was still human and couldn't
help but hate
To see the agony so clearly stamped on
His young face
On His way to die on Calvary for the
whole human race.

Though heartbroken, she stayed there as
long as she could
And wept, and prayed as any
good mother would.
I can imagine she had many thoughts as
she watched those men,
But she realized this must be done for
new life to begin.
Of course she would have sacrificed
herself that day,
But because of God's word it couldn't
happen that way.
Only her precious son could pay
that supreme price
Not anything less, in all the world, for
our sins would suffice.

Easter

E   is for the eagerness with which
      Christ came to save

A   is for the agony He suffered before
      going to the grave.

S   is for the sin that had the
      world so blind,

T   is for the tears He shed for the
      plight of mankind.

E   is for eternity He died that
      we might inherit

R   is for the righteousness which our
      lives could never merit.

The Beauty of Easter

Aren't the lilies beautiful at Eastertime,
Don't you love to hear the church bells chime?
They seem to sound sweeter and gently say,
Aren't you glad it's Easter day?

Guess Who

As I glanced down the road, who do
    you think I saw?

Why, the Easter bunny with a pretty new dress
    and hat of straw.

She came hip, hip hip, hopping
    so gaily along.

On her face was a smile and in her heart
    a glad Easter song.

Suppose

Suppose you had been one of the Shepherds in Bethlehem
long ago.
Suppose you had been seated as they and seen that
Heavenly glow.
And just suppose you had heard that Angelic Host singing
sweet and clear.
Can't you just imagine hearing their voices now and feel
their presence near?

Just suppose you had been with Mary when baby Jesus
was born,
And heard the cattle lowing on that peaceful morn.
Wouldn't it have been wonderful to have experienced
these blessed things?
I think if each of us had—we would be much better human
beings.

Christmas (I)

C   is for the Christchild born long ago.
H   is for the happiness He brought to our souls.
R   is for the right that Christians should display.
I   is for the innocence for which we pray.
S   is for our souls He came on earth to save.
T   is for the temple which for our benefit He raised.
M   is for Mary, blessed mother undefiled.
A   is for the Angels who with the shepherds did abide.
S   is for the sacredness that each year the occasion
    brings.
Put them all together they spell Christmas of which the
whole world sings.

Tired Elves

We are tired, tired elves, as tired
as we can be,
For all year long, we've been working
hard, you see,
To make things just right for good
girls and boys,
Repairing Santa's sleigh and making
brand new toys.
And now the sleigh is packed, and
loaded to the rim,
Just waiting for good old Santa
to deliver them.
As soon as the reindeer take off and over
the houses leap,
All that we'll be able to do is
sleep—sleep—sleep.

Christmas (II)

Christmas time is a great time—the best
    of all the year,
For everyone seems so happy and filled
    with love and cheer.
People rush around madly looking
    for pretty things,
Thinking of the joy and happiness that
    these presents bring.
Boys and girls are trying hard to do
    their very best,
For they realize that this is not the
    time to be a pest,
But the true meaning of Christmas, to all,
    should be very grave,
For it was then the Christchild came
    this world to save.

Try Smiling

A smile can dispel a heart that's
full of fear.

It can calm one's doubts and dry
many a tear.

A smile can lift a heart burdened
down with sorrow

And give you hope for a
brighter day tomorrow.

A smile can change a stubborn heart
to a heart of gold,

And cause a timid person to become
confident and bold.

A smile has changed many an argument to
a friendly conversation.

Often times in life have I made
this observation.

So try smiling—it certainly can't
hurt anything,

And who knows, it might add to
your life—zing.

Life (I)

L   is for the luxurious things which most of us can't
afford.
I   is for the numerous ills which many times obstruct
our goal.
F   is for the future which can always bring hope.
E   is for the energy we need to walk life's tight rope.
    Put them together and they spell life
    Filled with a little pleasure and a whole lot of strife.

Life (II)

Life is but a movie being shown on the screen,
With numerous varieties of good and bad scenes.
We play our respective parts and then go on
To receive our academy awards at the eternal throne.
And when our producer, who is God above,
Smiles down on us with His compassion and love,
We know that our performance has been what He
expected,
And from His "Eternal Stage" we will not be rejected.

Pleading

My blood cries out from the ground
For the many misdeeds encountered
by my brothers,
But I say to you, "Don't give up
the struggle
Or all my work will have been
in vain."

Smile

Smile, things aren't usually as bad
as they sometimes appear.
The world has enough sadness, try
spreading a little cheer.
A smile can spread sunshine and
dispel so many clouds of doubt.
It can soothe one's fears and bring
so much happiness about.
A smile can bring peace to an otherwise
bowed down heart.
It can bring pleasant memories, though
you're miles apart.
Just the thought of the smile of a
loved one or friend
Can help us to make the day and our
sadness bring to an end.

Love

Love makes little or no demands
    but gives of itself freely

To enhance the beauty of
    everything it touches.

It is not stubborn or rebellious
    and can adapt to changes without
    complaining.

Home

Home is more than just a place of retreat.
It's more than just a place to find something to eat.
It's more than just a place to shelter us from the cold,
Or to conveniently settle down when we get old.
It's more than a place for closing the world out,
Or to show off to friends and brag about.
It's more than just four walls regardless of how steady,
To dash in and out whenever we get ready.
It's more than just some convenient place
To escape all the troubles of life's rat race.
It's more than a place just to throw your hat,
Pull up a chair and talk about this and that.
Home is a place where we can share our troubles
And console one another when the problems come double.
It's a place where we can lie down and rest in peace
And from the cares of the day be calmly released.
It's a place where in each other we can confide.
It's the warmth that only a happy home can afford
When with the rest of the world we become bored.
It's a place of contentment, happiness, peace and love
That has been smiled upon by the Lord above.
Home is a place that will stand come what may
And bid us welcome there from day to day.

People

There are all kinds of people in our world today,
Yes, all kinds of people I can truthfully say,
For I've met many kinds as I went about my tasks
And to find what kind they were I didn't have to ask.
I've seen happy people who wanted everyone to be glad;
I've seen gloomy people who enjoyed making others sad.
I've seen people who plot, lie, cheat and steal;
I've seen people whose lives have never been real,
People who rejoice when they see a fellowman lost
And aspire to get ahead in the world, at any cost.
There are people who will do anything for money;
People who, for some reason, think everything is funny.
There are people who will do anything that pleases them
And expect everyone to bow and cater to their childlike
whims.
Then there are people who are sweet, sincere and kind,
Humble of heart and soul and sober of mind,
People who will meet you more than halfway,
People who will come to your rescue night or day.
Which of these people are you, do you know?
Don't kid yourself, sooner or later it will show.

I've Learned to Be Content

(From Philippians)

I've learned to be content in whatever
    state I'm found,
For like Paul, I learned to be abased and
    I've learned to abound.
I've learned that this life has
    no picks and chooses,
For sometimes man wins but many
    more times he loses.
A brief time we're happy but much
    more often, we're sad.
Some decisions we make are good,
    but many more are bad.
A wonderful ray of sunshine is all too soon
    covered with clouds of doubt,
And our lives, like ships on a stormy sea,
    are furiously tossed about,
But I've learned to be still and
    let God take full control,
For in my life, He now truly
    has the leading role.
There have been times when I had plenty
    and was happy and gay,
Then at other times I didn't have a dime
    but felt the same way,
Just knowing in my heart that
    Jesus was always there,
To sustain me at all times and
    keep me in His care.

What Is Life?

Life to the gambler is only
another game,
Life to the baseball player is
just the same.
Life to the surgeon is another
successful operation,
Life to the attorney is another
consultation.
Life to the singer is another
successful song,
Life to the criminal is doing
something wrong.
Life to the teacher is another
lesson taught,
Life to the soldier is another
battle fought.
Life to the reporter is an exciting
story told,
Life to the archaeologist is finding
skeletons of old.
Life to the scientist is another
discovery great,
Life to each gender is satisfying
his or her mate.
Life to the sprinter is another
great run,
Life to the foolish is just a
time for fun.
Life to the creditor is trying to
collect a bill,
Life to the despondent always seems
to be uphill.

Life to the cobbler is making another
pair of shoes,
Life to the union member is paying
up the dues.
Life to the horticulturist is developing
a lovely rose
Life to the model is working for the right pose
Life to the minister is an effective
sermon preached,
Life to the mountain climber is another
height reached.
Life to the rich man is building
up his wealth,
Life to the sick is praying
for good health.
Life to the farmer is tilling
of the soil,
Life to the poor man seems a
constant toil.
Life to the pilot is completing
a successful flight,
Life to the complainer is another
sad plight.
Life to the alcoholic is just
another drink,
Life to the skater is another
big rink.
Life to the real estate agent is another
house sold,
Life to the miner is prospecting for gold.
Life to the artist is beauty
beyond compare,
Life to the young is a great
love affair.

Life to someone weary is getting
a little rest,
Life to the student is passing
another test.
Life to someone hungry is just
getting his fill,
But life to the Christian is
doing God's will.

Daniel

(*From the Bible*)

According to the Scriptures, Daniel was
        a righteous man,
And for the God in whom he believed
        boldly took a stand.
His character was spotless, according
        to what we read,
And his entire life must have been filled
        with good deeds.
Gabriel referred to Daniel as a man
        beloved of God,
For he knew to Daniel God was
        his staff and rod.
The devil tried to keep him from
        saying his prayers,
But Daniel knew the devil couldn't
        handle God's affairs.
He prayed three times a day in
        spite of the decree,
For he was rooted and grounded in
        God's love, you see.

And when he was cast into the lion's den,
    Daniel didn't fret,
For he knew that the God he served hadn't
    failed him yet,
So he went into the den like a soldier
    brave and true
And God stepped in and did what
    He had to do.
The lions didn't attack Daniel as
    the devil expected,
For God would not, in any wise, have
    His will rejected.
These ferocious lions, some of the
    wildest in the land,
Walked around meekly and just
    licked Daniel's hand.
Now this seemed odd to sinners, but
    all Christians know,
That it is true because the Bible
    tells us so.

All of Us Are Guilty

Each of us is guilty of one thing
    or another,
Of doing things, though unconsciously, against
    and to each other.
We're guilty of the sins of omission and
    of commission too
Regardless of how careful we are in what
    we say and do.

We're guilty of saying things that would
        be better unsaid,
We're guilty of living as husband and wife
        even though unwed.
We're guilty of going places that a
        Christian shouldn't go,
And doing things ungodly because we think
        no one else will know.
We're guilty of giving to the very ones
        who are not in need,
And neglecting the hungry sheep that Christ
        told us to feed.
We're guilty of not paying our tithes
        offerings and gifts,
Of not being kind because someone's
        spirit it lifts.
We're guilty of being quiet when we
        know we should speak,
And letting that secret out that we
        promised someone we'd keep.
So many of us are guilty of
        falling from grace,
And stabbing someone in the back while
        smiling in his/her face.
Yes, all of us are guilty of something as
        we live from day to day.
It isn't always what we do but
        often what we say,
But just remember while your're pointing
        that finger at me,
Take a look, for pointing back
        at you are three.

In Tune with God

When your life is not in tune with God,
you're in the danger zone,

And in a time of crisis, you'll
find yourself out their alone.

When your life is not in tune with God,
no true happiness you'll find.

You'll wander to and fro, searching
diligently for peace of mind.

On the outside, to others, everything
seems to be all right,

But on the inside, a constant battle
you'll be trying to fight.

You frolic about day in and out and
from place to place you roam,

But when you find yourself in need and
look around, everyone is gone.

When you start out, everything seems great
and you feel like a millionaire,

But just get down to your last dime
and you'll find out how many care.

Then you'll begin to wonder what happened,
I used to have friends galore,

But as soon as I got down on my luck,
they all walked out the door.

Then as you sit and ponder your situation,
it will gradually dawn on you

There's something wrong in my life and
I need to find out what to do.

Then you'll remember a God that your
mother used to teach you about,

And you begin to think to yourself, maybe
it's because I've left Him out.

So you begin to talk to Him in earnest
and He knows you're sincere.

He's listening and will answer, for
He is always near.

Then you'll begin a prayer life and
watch as well as pray,

And commit yourself to seriously
studying the Bible every day.

Then you'll find out what it is
that God wants of you

And you'll find yourself striving to do
whatever it is He wants you to.

Before you realize it, you'll find yourself
working day and night until

Your main objective on this earth will be
to do the Master's will.

Then you'll have a complete new outlook
as upon this earth you trod,

For at last you've come to the realization
that your life is in tune with God.

It doesn't mean that you won't have
problems, that's part of a Christian's life,

To encounter difficulties and carry
your share of troubles and strife—

David said, "Many are the afflictions of the righteous,
but the Lord delivereth him out of them all."

So when your life is in tune with God, in
the face of adversity, you will pray and stand tall.

Pseudo-Christianity

Some of us go to church on Sunday,
we sing, jump and shout,

But we really don't know what
Christianity is all about.

We sit through the service and
sometimes we fellowship,

But on each of our shoulders we
oftentimes carry a chip.

We criticize the sermon and say
it was just too long,

And that the choir didn't sing
a single good song.

We criticize the stewards because
they ask for money,

As we get so tickled because
someone's clothes look funny.

We complain about the musician,
though we can't play a note

And criticize announcements that
the secretary wrote.

We accuse the ushers of not
doing their job right,

And if anyone says something to us,
we're ready for a fight.

If we're asked to do a job, we
very quickly decline,

Yet when someone else does it,
we sit at home and pine.

We talk about the mothers and how the
Lord's table they serve

And if something goes wrong, we'll say
they got what they deserve.

We are so envious of others who
seem to be getting ahead,

We lie on the living and tell
lies for the dead.

We turn so many people off because
of the way we live,

That they feel it's no use their
lives to Christ give.

But this is not how true Christianity
was designed to be

Christ, himself set the example on earth
for both you and me.

He was not only kind and humble,
but He was also meek,

And He forgave his oppressors and
cared for the weak.

He continued to pray for those
who despitefully used Him,

And blessed those who cursed
and abused Him.

So if Christian perfection we
ever hope to gain,

We must follow in Christ's footsteps
or life will be in vain.

No, we'll never be really perfect,
never as perfect as He,

But we can be as perfect as we
lowly mortals can be.

So pull off that pseudo-Christianity—turn
to Christ and do your best.

If and when you do, don't worry,
He'll take care of the rest.

Dusk to Dawn

When the bountiful sky spreads its
  blanket of darkness
O'er the earth's troubles and trials
  of the day
And the peaceful serenity of evening
  shadows are cast,
We lie down to drink in the beauty
  of the night
And forget the troubles which today
  seemed so vast.
When the twinkling stars light
  up the heavens
And reflect a beautiful light down
  upon the earth,
My mind wanders back to an event
  of long, long ago

When Mary gave to the world a grand
    and noble birth.
When the sun rises each morning
    shining bright and clear
And the ground with midnight dew
    is soaking wet,
I'm reassured day after day that
    God is always near
And I have no reason at all
    to worry or fret.

We Pass This Way Once

We pass this way but once
    and then,
Our lives on this earth will come
    to an end.
We have no time at all
    to waste,
For this life as we know it is passing
    with haste.
We don't have time to argue,
    fuss and fight.
We need each day to try to do
    what is right.
We need to walk together talk together
    watch and pray,
And seek God's guidance for our
    lives each day,
We don't have a chance to undo what
    we have done,
So do it right the first time before
    each setting sun.

T   is for the times of suffering
     that the Pilgrims had,

H   is for the hard times that came
     when crops were bad.

A   is for the anticipation they had
     from year to year,

N   is for the needs they had and
     disappointments and fear.

K   is the kindness they showed as ofttimes
     with each other they cried,

S   is for the sorrow they encountered
     when so many died.

G   is for the gifts they know God had
     in store for them,

I   is for the indescribable faith that
     they had in Him.

V   is for the victory that they knew
     someday would be theirs,

I   is for the immense blessings they
     thanked Him for in their prayers.

N   is for the neophytes they were
     in this land so new,

G   is for gratitude to God for protection
     and seeing them through.

Consolation

Heavy-hearted and sad, I sat feeling so alone,
Things seemed hopeless and all my strength was gone.
I cared not that others had felt this pain
That I now felt as their loved ones were lain
In the cold, dark earth underneath the sod,
For it was their time to give an account to God.
I thought not of all the happy times we'd had.
All I could think of was now I was very sad.
My selfish desire was to keep my loved one here
Where we could with one another always be near.
I thought not of the days of suffering and the nights of
pain,
When all she longed for was that better life to gain.
But as I listened to the message by the minister said,
I dried my eyes and slowly lifted my head,
For he brought so many beautiful things to mind,
And caused me to think, relax and slowly unwind.
I thought of how happy my loved one must be
To at last be gone with Christ to spend eternity.
So now I'm happy that at last her suffering is done.
For her, life's battle has been fought and her victory won.

In Times Like These

In times like these we need women with power,
Women who will stand for right every day and hour.
Women who will not faint though pressed by every foe,
Women who will lift Christ up wherever they go.
Women who won't retreat in the face of disaster,
Women who are willing to work daily for the Master.
Women who will not let their virtue trail in the dust,
Women who will not betray a fellowman's trust.

In times like these, we need women of truth,
Not immoral women who are foolish and uncouth.
Women whose characters are not questionable and weak,
Women who have convictions and will boldly speak
Against the wiles of the devil and sins of man,
Even though they, from life socially, may be banned.

In times like these, we need women with ambitions to be
Carbon copies, dear Heavenly Father, of Thee.
Women with desires to do all that they should,
To be guiding lights in their own neighborhoods.
Women like these, even in times like these, can be
produced
When they let Christ guide them and of their talents
make use.

Thank You, God

Thank you, God, for your love
so pure,

Thank you, God, for patience with
us to endure.

Thank you, God, for wonderful and
gentle rain

That swiftly falls upon our
window pane.

Thank you, God, for the lilies of
the field,

Thank you, God, for the bounty by
the earth yield.

Thank you, God, for your love
and your care,

Thank you, God, for the clothes
we wear.

Thank you, God, for the grass and
for the flowers,

Thank you, God, for this beautiful
world of ours.

Thank you, God, for joy and thank
you for sorrow,

Thank you, God, for the hope
for tomorrow.

Thank you, God, for our eyes
with which to see,

Thank you, God, for a mind
to worship Thee.

Thank you, God, for the birds on
our window sill,

Thank you, God, for helping us to
do Thy will.

Thank you, God, for our feet that
can walk for Thee.

Thank you for letting me
your servant be.

Thank you, God, for the food
that we eat.

Thank you, God, for the corn
and the wheat.

Thank you, God, for the sorrow
now passed away,

Thank you, God, for each blessing
day after day.

Thank you, God, for the clothes
we wear,

Thank you, God, for keeping me
in your care.

Thank you, God, for watching daily
over me,

Thank you for moving the stumbling
blocks I can't see.

Thank you, God, for moving on the
altar of my heart,

Thank you, God, for giving me
a brand new start.

Thank you, God, for the hurt by others
sent my way,

Thank you, God, for hearing me
when I pray.

Thank you, God, for guidance as I
walk this road,

Thank you, God, for helping me to
bear my load.

Thank you, God, for Jesus, your
precious son,

Thank you for the pain he endured and
the victory he won.

Thank you, God, for strength
and health,

Thank you, God, for blessing me with
spiritual wealth.

Thank you, God, for the love of friends
gone before,

Thank you, God, for my parents
whom I adore.

Thank you, God, for the children entrusted
in my care,

Thank you, God, for every burden that I've
had to bear.

Thank you, God, for everything
you do,

Thank you, God, for just
being you.

Beyond the Horizon

Way over the blue horizon in a
land yet unknown,
Our merciful Father is standing watch
awaiting His own.
Beyond the blue horizon where only
immortals dwell
Are precious gifts eternal that only
time will tell.

Beyond the blue horizon where time will
cease to be,
Where joy will reign forever and spirits
will run free.
Beyond the blue horizon is peace from
cares and woe,
The kind of peace that this world
will never know.

Beyond the blue horizon we'll sing an
everlasting song
Where right will be the byword and no
place for wrong.
Beyond the blue horizon where someday
I shall be,
Rejoicing with all my loved ones who're
waiting there for me.

Talent

Whatever talent you have, don't fail
    to use it,
For if you do, you can rest assured
    you'll lose it.
You might think it very insignificant and
    having no appeal,
But how will you know unless you nourish it
    if that talent is real?
It might not turn heads around you or
    set the world aspin
Or cause some great writer a
    lavish work to pen,
But whatever your talent—work at it and
    it will get better
And whether it be great or small just
    be a go-getter.

A Good Layman

A good layman is a person who
is very unique,
For he knows when to refrain and just
when to speak.
He is always sensitive to his
fellowman's needs,
And will do everything in his power to
help the church succeed.
A good layman doesn't pout because he
can't have his way,

But his life reflects Christ each and
every day.
He certainly would not try to take
advantage of anyone,
And tries to do things just as Christ
would have done.
He speaks boldly, but not haughty
selfish or unkind,
For he always has the welfare of others
uppermost in his mind.
A good layman works with the pastor
and respects him too,
And in the midst of confusion, does
what he has to do.
He gives not only his tithes, but
his talent and his time,
And for right, will put not only his reputation,
but his life on the line.
A good layman doesn't stir up confusion or
meddle in the lives of others,
But tries to treat all of God's children
as sisters and brothers.
Though not a minister, he too is
called by God,
To meet the challenge of working in
the Christian vineyard.
Sure he has problems and sorrows, just
as Jesus has said,
But no way would he trample on another
just to get ahead.
He stands as tall timber in the midst
of misery and strife,
For he knows that someday he'll
exchange it for a better life.

Be Patient

Be patient, you too were once young
and very headstrong,
And with your own parents you
didn't always get along.
You didn't always take heed
to what they told you
And so many times through the years
they had to scold you.
You were not always the epitome of
obedience and good,
For many times you did things they didn't like
just because you could.
You said things that would hurt your
parents if they knew what you said.
You went along with your peers when
you knew you were being misled.
You made it this far, don't kid yourself,
not on your own,
But by the prayers of others some of whom
are now gone home.

Be patient, the world was not
made in a day.
It takes time to develop, especially
in a Christian way.
Don't be so quick to point a
finger and criticize,
Talk about the shortcomings of
others and ostracize.
Don't act like you've always
done what God would have you do,
For He knows and is keeping
a record on me and you.

Be patient, we all need to have
time in which to grow
Into the responsible people that
we want others to know.

PART TWO

WELCOMES, INTRODUCTIONS, AND RESPONSES

Welcome   (I)

As the flowers welcome the morning dew, as the dry earth welcomes the refreshing rain, as a mother welcomes a long-lost daughter, as the father of the Prodigal Son welcomed him home with outstretched arms—so we welcome you here today.

Your attendance here today verifies the fact that we share a common bond of fellowship. There are so many other places you could have gone. I'm sure you were extended other invitations, but you chose to share this hour with us and we want you to know that we appreciate your coming.

So sit back, relax and enjoy the program that we have worked so hard to prepare for your entertainment. We trust that it will be time well spent. And remember, you're always welcome, so please come again.

Welcome (II)

To the Mistress or Master of Ceremonies, most illustrious pastor, platform guests, officers, members and visiting friends, it makes my heart rejoice to see you here today.

It is always like a family reunion whenever brothers and sisters gather together in our Father's house. Here we are free to sing, meditate, rejoice, and fellowship with one another.

Remember, you don't have to wait for a special occasion or an invitation. Come as you are and whenever you have an opportunity. Our doors are always open to anyone who desires to come—today, tomorrow and always—indeed you are welcome.

Welcome (III)

Welcome, Christian friends, from the
greatest to the small,

We extend a heartfelt welcome to you
one and all.

After all, our house is your Father's
house too,

So it really isn't necessary to stand here
and welcome you.

But age-old customs sometimes require
us to do

Many things, out of love, though we really
don't need to.

For if your Father is our Father, then we are
sisters and brothers,

And it is our Christian duty to
greet one another.

We hope your visit here will be
a pleasant one,

And to assure that it is—everything in our
power will be done.

There are so many other places you could
have been today,

But you chose to visit us and we want you to
have a happy stay,

So join in with us and help
us to celebrate,

And leave so filled with joy that to return
you can't wait.

Again we're so glad you came and want
you to come back,

And we promise that our enthusiasm
will never be slack.

Introduction of a Speaker

(Woman)

My heart is overflowing with joy as I stand here to
introduce this great person. She is endowed with such
grace, talent, beauty, both inside and out, that words
sufficient to describe her seem to evade me at this time.

However, I'll share a few of her outstanding qualities
with you, and by the time I shall have finished, you will
be filled with anticipation for the treat that lies in store
for you. Her personality will be indelibly stamped in your
memory.

This person is the kind that was spoken of in the poem "The Bridge Builder," for she has built many bridges over which so many others have passed, and held a light high enough so that others may not stumble as they follow in her footsteps, and yet low enough that even a little child following will not lose the way.

She is a lady in every sense of the word. She commands the respect of all men, and at the same time, with adoration and praise of other women.

I could go on and on describing this colorful individual because of her numerous talents. Instead, I'll give to you now the person you've been anxiously awaiting. Ladies and gentlemen, I present to you the speaker for the evening———

Introduction of a Speaker

(Man)

As I stand before this vast audience in awe, I feel inadequate to perform the task that has been assigned me—that of presenting your speaker of the hour, for he possesses so many talents and has encountered so many unique experiences.

He is the kind of person who can mingle with kings and potentates and yet enjoy the fellowship of all men, even those beneath his intellectual and social status. He asks not of others, what can you do for me, but rather what can I do to help you?

He possesses the sensitivity to hear the cries of the hopeless, the eloquence to attract the attention of men in high places, the fortitude to venture into new and challenging avenues and yet, that down-to-earth, genuine friendliness that makes one feel at ease in his presence.

Ladies and gentlemen, I could go on indefinitely describing the wonderful characteristics of this person—but because you have waited so patiently and because I know what a wonderful treat you have in store, I will not keep you wainting any longer. So, lest I infringe upon his time, I present your speaker for the evening, Mr.————.

Response (I)

To the Master of Ceremonies, pastor, officers, and members of this great church and all who go to make up this great body of Christian believers, I am indeed happy to be here today. My heart was strangely warmed as I listened to those beautiful words of welcome so graciously extended by ————.

Even though words of welcome are not necessary, they certainly give us a sense of belonging. So, on behalf of all the visitors in attendance here today, I accept those wonderful words of welcome in the same warm spirit in which they were extended.

To the young lady/gentleman who just yielded the floor, don't stop here. Go out into the highways and hedges and continue to welcome others into the vineyard. Then, one day, when your assignment in this world is finished, our Heavenly Father will extend to you a welcome to His kingdom where you'll be able to spend an eternity with Him.

Response (II)

It is with humble and heartfelt gratitude that I stand in your presence to accept for all visitors in attendance here today your most gracious and sincere welcome.

The beautiful words of greeting were like a cool drink of water after a long, hot journey; like the warm breath of spring after cold winter nights, like a friendly arrow that gently pierced our hearts with love, like a mother with outstretched arms to greet a wayward child returning home.

Your lovely smiles, friendly handshakes, and pleasant nods have made us all glad we came.

So may I say sincerely, on behalf of all visitors, we accept those warm words of welcome in the same genuine spirit in which they were offered.

To the young lady who did such a beautiful job extending the welcome, don't stop, but continue to work for the Master and welcome others into His vineyard. Then one day you'll hear that welcome voice saying to you, "Well done, My good and faithful servant. You have been faithful over a few things on earth—come up higher and I'll make you ruler over many."

May God bless you.

PART THREE
ADDRESSES

Check Your Heart Out

(*Address*)

Once we accept Christ, Paul said that we must accept His command to love thy neighbor as thyself. We now have an obligation to our fellowman, which we never had before—the obligation to serve. We can no longer live under the selfish law—I made it on my own, he can too. But rather, we are willing to serve God through serving mankind. This is an everyday job, for if we are not constantly aware of this, we can easily slip back into that nonchalant day-to-day existence where we project self. We must not let this happen if we are going to be able to reach spiritual maturity.

Let us take a true-life situation. In each of our homes, there are cabinets or pantries in which we store food for both present and future consumption. Every so often, the housewife will check it out in order to see what needs restocking and what needs to be thrown out. In other words, sometimes we find that we have accumulated so much junk that is virtually worthless that we don't have room to stock the necessities. So as a result, what do we do? We commence to clean out this storage space in order to make room for the commodities we need to sustain our physical well-being from day to day.

This is an ideal time to do the spring cleaning in the cabinets and pantries of our hearts and restock them. This is the only way we'll be able to proceed successfully with the work we, as followers of Christ, have contracted to do. Where we are overstocked with hate and malice, let Christ restock it with love and mercy. He has an abundant supply of both. Where there is confusion, restock it with peace. Where there is petty jealousy, restock it with sincere praise. Where there is impatience, restock it with endurance. Where there is disrespect, replace it with honor. Where there is indifference, replace it with concern. Letting others know that you care can turn their whole lives around. You see, when we take inventory of our lives and work to improve our images spiritually, physically, socially and intellectually, we not only help others but ourselves also.

You might say, "I am not envious, and I don't harbor hatred and malice in my heart." But we can always make a little more room for the aforementioned commodities that will tend to sustain us and keep us near the cross. Keep in mind that Romans 3:12 says, "There is none that doeth good, no not one." So let us not become complacent and self-righteous.

After having checked out, thrown out, then stocked and restocked the cabinets and pantries of our hearts with all the necessary virtues to enhance our Christian lives, let us then use these things to the best advantage with the welfare of our fellowman always uppermost in our minds.

Many millionaires have died of malnutrition. So it can be with us. We can be equipped with all the necessities and still, by not using them daily, die of spiritual malnutrition. Being aware of all this and possessing all of these qualities and not using them is just as bad as not having them at all.

So check your heart out. A physical heart that is not functioning properly, can be detrimental to our health. A spiritual heart that is overloaded with ungodly qualities is detrimental to our spiritual growth. Keep constant check on both, for out of them flow the issues of life.

Take a Look at Your Insurance Coverage

(*Address*)

As I sat with my husband one day listening to a great sales pitch by a well-informed insurance agent, my mind kept wandering from the conversation. It was not that I wasn't interested in what was being said, but an insurance policy that this young man was not qualified to write kept running through my mind.

In the course of the presentation, I learned quite a bit about the various policies being offered by this company, which, by the way, is one of the most reputable in the business.

As the representative talked incessantly, giving both facts and figures regarding the assets of his company, I became fascinated by his sincerity. He was really sold on this company. He believed, without a doubt, that this was the best insurance company in the world and it offered coverage suited to any need that might arise regarding life and death benefits.

As most women will do, I asked many questions about the company, the age of the company, stability, ethnic representation, the promptness regarding payment of claims, validity of the policies including the small print, etc.

The agent did not become hostile, nervous, or aggravated because of all the inquiries; rather, he was very patient and thorough. He encouraged us to ask any questions we desired, for he was able to answer any of them with little or no hesitation. He did not exaggerate or promise more than his company could perform.

My husband, who is a quiet but observant person, asked some pertinent questions that never crossed my

175

mind. He was concerned about the legal wording in policies, which make it complicated for most lay persons to interpret. We found that this company tried to be fair with its clients, and the policies were so written that anyone with a reasonable degree of intelligence and/or common sense could both read and understand the policy.

In the process of the conversation, we found that this company offered practically any kind of policy anyone would ever need. The educational policy, we learned, was just great for our little boy who has college ahead of him. The endowment policy was what we agreed on for our daughter because even though she is married and has a lovely daughter of her own, we realized that this would be a help to her someday. Then we decided that we should avail ourselves of the opportunity to increase our life insurance, for we would not want to die and leave a financial burden on our children along with the grief that comes at that time.

Realizing that sickness could strike at any time and hospital costs have skyrocketed and since accidents happen at the most unexpected times, we knew that hospitalization, sick and accident policies were a must. We even considered the health policy and made some small investments for our twilight years. We now felt very secure and had insured the security of our children. But in the back of my mind, something kept gnawing inside me. For you see, even though we had all this protection, I knew of another policy that my family needed and possessed whose value is greater than any company on this earth could offer.

This insurance of which I speak is the assurance that John 3:16 give us: "For God so loved the world that He gave His only begotten Son, that whosoever believeth on Him shall not perish, but have everlasting life." This

policy was taken out over nineteen hundred years ago
and made available to everyone, without cost, through
the blood of Jesus. The agent, Jesus, stands at the door
of your heart, knocking and pleading. He won't force His
way in, just as our earthly insurance agent did not, but
He waits for you to invite Him in. He will then enter and
the joy that you'll have will be greater than any known.

Jesus is the world's greatest agent and knows
everything about this Celestial policy, which covers every
aspect of life, not only on this earth, but life after death
also. There is no small print to trick you. This policy is
the Holy Bible.

The dividends are the highest that can be paid. On
the life policies here on earth, only the beneficiary can
profit from the life insurance. But, in the policy issued
by Jesus, not only you gain eternal life, but your
beneficiary as well, if he or she takes advantage of the
policy as outlined in the Scriptures.

The premiums are so structured that even the poorest
person in the world can afford them. In this life, if we do
not pay our premiums within a given period of time, the
policy will lapse (ending of rights, benefits, etc., through
failure to fill certain conditions of the policy), thereby
losing all monies paid thereon and cancelling said
coverage. Then there are policies where the value
diminishes as we grow older. Some are even cancelled or
phased out totally after a certain age, and we cannot take
out new ones.

But with the policy that Jesus Christ offers, there is
no age limit—and no lapsing. We can always sincerely
ask forgiveness and become reinstated with no penalty
inflicted. We don't lose any benefits because of age for
the policy clearly states: The race is not given to the swift
nor to the strong, but he that endureth to the end.

The most important thing to do is to make up your mind that in order to inherit eternal life, this coverage is a must! The first premium is to love the Lord thy God with all thy heart, soul, mind, and strength. The second premium is to love your neighbor as yourself. Following the other commandments daily that Christ gave will insure permanent coverage. There's no need to worry about cancellation on the part of the insuror.

Just as we have to adhere to the terms of our insurance policy (man-made), we must adhere to the terms stipulated in our contract with Christ and just as we take those policies out from time to time and look over them in order to reassure ourselves we have sufficient coverage and check to see that our payment books are up to date, so we must check out our lives from time to time to see if we are keeping the terms of our Christian policy. This is the only way we can receive the dividends outlined in the Holy Scriptures.

Harvest Day

(Address)

Webster defines 'harvest' as the act of gathering a crop of grain or fruit, etc., when it becomes ripe or the time of year when a crop is gathered. In practically every country in the world, a numerous variety of crops are planted and harvested each year. Man tills the soil, plants the seeds, and then nature takes its course.

The Bible makes more than twenty references to the harvest, the first one being Genesis 8:22, which reads:

"While the earth remaineth, seed time and harvest and heat and cold and summer and winter and day and night shall not cease" (KJV). Proverbs 10:5 states, "He that gathereth in summer is a wise son; but he that sleepth in harvest is a son that causeth shame." This brings about the question—why would anyone bother to plant a crop when they know no intention is planned to harvest it? Jeremiah 8:20 states, "The harvest is past, the summer ended and we are not saved." All of these Scriptures are in different connotations, but Matthew 9:37 says, "So He said to His disciples, the harvest is large, but there are few workers to gather it in."

So you see, fellow Christians, this is a challenge for us today. For even though those words were spoken many hundreds of years ago, they are still relevant today. Out in the fields of life ready for harvesting are the lives of boys and girls, men and women. Their very lives are hanging in the balance, waiting for us to come and gather them into the Christian fold.

When you go out to harvest crops of corn, peas, potatoes, cotton, fruit or whatever, one must have some knowledge about what he or she is doing because it takes various skills to harvest certain crops. Some produce is so delicate that unless we know just what we're doing, the crop could be ruined. The same goes for the kind of harvesting Jesus was talking about. We must be prepared by studying the Bible and praying for the skill we need before going out to harvest boys and girls, men and women. Some of the equipment that is a necessity is putting on the breastplate of righteousness and having our feet shod with the preparation of the gospel. We must have the necessary skill because out there in the fields of life, the wheat and tares grow together, and without it, we might get the wheat and tares confused. They can be so entangled that our frail minds could tend to make the harvesting disastrous. Matthew 3:30 says, "Let both grow together until the harvest; and in the time of harvest, I will say to the reapers—gather ye first the tares and bind them in bundles to burn then gather the wheat into my barn."

We have so-called Christians whose lives are so interwined with those of sinners until it is difficult to tell which is which. It is not our job to judge them, but to do everything out there in the field of life for the upbuilding of God's kingdom. Then, on that great day, our Heavenly Father will be the reaper; you'll hear that welcome voice say—"Well done, good and faithful servant. Enter the storehouse that I prepared for you from the foundation of the world."

The Star of Bethlehem

(*Address*)

When the word star is mentioned, we usually think of definitions given by Webster, Thorndike Barnhart, or some other authoritative source—some of which might be:

1. Star—any of the heavenly bodies appearing as bright points in the sky at night.
2. Any heavenly body except the moon, the planets, comets and meteors.
3. A plane figure having five points.
4. A person who is distinguished in some art, profession, or other field.
5. A heavenly body considered as influencing people and events.

I could go on and on with definitions given by many great minds regarding the word star.

The greatest star, to the Wise Men or astronomers, was perhaps the one they saw many years ago that shone so brightly and led them to the Christ child. Little did these men realize that baby Jesus would be the world's greatest star with performances that could not be comprehended by the greatest minds of men. This star, Jesus, was one that mere mortals would not have the capability of describing, for His performance while here on earth outshone the brightest star in the heavens and that of any human who ever endeavored to portray a star in the secular realm.

All of us at one time or another watched persons regarded as starts in their particular fields on television. We've seen many of them nominated for and receive various awards for superb performances and rightfully so because they were skilled in their professions. Some have been the envy of others for having received such recognition.

There are many biblical references regarding the word 'star' with explanations for the same. Each of us could, no doubt, expound upon the word.

I read in Jennie Broadnax Vance's book of a woman whose ambition was to be a big recognized missionary— and as the story goes this, woman was anxious to reach the top, anxious to be rated among the best loved. She wanted to be the star, and was willing to pay the price, so she thought. Her aim was to be the star of the great missionary field. With determination she kept an ever-watchful eye on her star. She tried hard every day to come nearer to her goal. She'd strive to pay the largest amount, lead in any drive, and be looked upon as great.

As time went on, the distance between her and her

goal seemed to grow further away. She was playing the role of the big shot, but her heart still felt barren. People regarded her in the position, but that was all. The star upon which she kept a vigilant eye became an elusive dream.

In the face of seeming defeat, she bowed her head in despair, realizing she had not triumphed in winning her way into the hearts of the masses. As she bowed her head for the first time in a long while, there about her feet were little children needing her guidance—children whom she'd had no time to see. Because her eyes were always on the stars and the fascination of that distant scene, she could not hear the cries of her fellowman, she couldn't see their eyes, the despair in their hearts. There were those before her eyes whose lives needed charting, some needed adjustments to their surroundings, and some who had never heard the word of God. Well, the woman, as the story goes, shruddered in disgust as this realization came upon her. Here, at her feet, was the ladder of love that extended to the hearts of all men. Here was the bright star of her life, the chance to tell the world about a star, to help them find their way to Him, and to show them by her life, how He loved the least of these. She had at last found a real star—the only star.

We often think of a star as having five or six points. But I would like to introduce the star of my life—the star that has unlimited points, a few which I will address at this time.

The first point in the star of Bethlehem is that of Love—love that has no bounds, is not selfish, is not turned on when pleased and turned off when displeased. Paul, in his first letter to the Corinthians, put it so beautifully when he said, and I quote, "Though I speak with the tongues of men and of angels and have not charity (love)

I am become as a sounding brass or a tinkling cymbal. And though I have all faith so that I could remove mountains and have not charity (love) I am nothing. Charity suffereth long and is kind, love envieth not; vaunt not itself, is not puffed up." That is true unadulterated love—the kind exemplified by the star of Bethlehem.

The second point I would like to think of as Mercy. Mercy can be described as kind treatment or mildness where severity is expected or deserved—or the power to show kindness or pity. But the star of Bethlehem's mercy is more in depth than this. This mercy was exemplified to a thief dying on the cross who asked for it. He shows that same mercy for each of us today. All we have to do is a little reminiscing. Think of the sins of both omission as well as commission we've committed. We can't help, as Christians, being grateful for the kind of mercy only He gives so freely. All we have to do is what the song writer says, "Come to the mercy seat, fervently kneel; Here bring your wounded heart, here tell your anguish— Earth has no sorrow that Heaven cannot heal."

Then let's think of the next point as Patience—being able to wait for someone or something—to endure unpleasant situations without complaining. Only the star of Bethlehem can help us to acquire this patience. Being human, we tend to want things and want them to happen right now or whenever we want them to happen. This does not always happen, but if we keep our eyes on that star, it will give us the stamina to endure. One portion of the Scripture says, "They that wait upon the Lord shall renew their strength. They shall mount up on wings as eagles. They shall run and not be weary, they shall walk and not faint. Teach us, Lord, how to wait."

I shall behold Him but not now; There shall come a star out of Jacob, and a Sceptre shall rise out of Israel

and shall smite the corners of Moab, and destroy all the
children of Sheth; out of Jacob shall come he that shall
have dominion and shall destroy him that remaineth in
the city."

Lest I confuse you by the use of the above reference
to Jacob in the previous verses, let me hasten to remind
you that Jacob, the grandson of Abraham, is a member
of the ancestral line through which Jesus Christ the Son
of David came.

In the 22nd Chapter of Revelation, verse 16, we find
these words: "I, Jesus, have sent mine angel to testify
unto you these things in the churches. I am the root and
offspring of David and the bright and morning star."

Today, we recognize and acknowledge as Christians
that Star of Bethlehem, Jesus who came to earth more
than two thousand years ago to redeem us from the curse
of sin and Satan.

As I look out over this beautiful world God made and
see so many wicked and sinful people, so much poverty,
hunger, sickness, loneliness, drug-addicted human
beings experiencing every form of suffering and deprava-
tion, all I can say, like the saints of old, is Oh, Thou Star
of David, Have mercy, Lord.

He came to the world in the most humble manner a
child has ever come—not because He had that to do, but
to show both you and me the way of humility; to let us
know that if we stay in touch with Him and do His
bidding, He'll be there in the lonely hours. He'll be our
company-keeper when we are burdened. He'll be our
friend when all have turned their backs on us. When we
feel we just can't go on, just look to that Star of David—
Jesus—and He will quicken our footsteps.

Listen reverently to the sounds of the hymnologist
as he says, "Come ye disconsolate—where'er ye lan-

guish—Come to the mercy seat, fervently kneel; Here bring your wounded heart, here tell your anguish, earth has no sorrow that Heaven cannot heal." He's still standing with outstretched arms today saying to each of us, "Lo, I am with you always, even to the end of the world."

So as the yuletide season approaches, let us not get hung up on gift-swapping and all the gala and commercialism that goes along with it. Let's keep our eyes on the star, the Star of Bethlehem. He's there. I know He's there waiting to be invited into our lives to make them full in the truest sense and extent of the word.

Bethlehem's Star

Star of stars—O Bethlehem star,
What a wondrous light you are.
You're the light that leads me on,
Whether I'm with friends or all alone.
Even when I'm tempted to go astray,
You're there shining to point the way.
I dare not take my eyes off thee,
Or the dangers around me I would not see.
So shine on, star of Bethlehem, that I will know
The right direction in which my life should go.

PART FOUR

TRIBUTES AND EULOGIES

A Tribute to Our Boss

(John Renick)

All of our hats are off to you on
this bosses' day,
For you have truly exemplified uniqueness
in every possible way.
You're always there for us whenever
you are needed,
To point out mistakes and praise us
when we've succeeded.
You're the epitome of honesty, fairness,
and common sense, too,
And without your wisdom we would
not know what to do.
In spite of the pressure from
the Board of Education,
You go about calmy in handling
any situation.
You breezed through the renovation
as no one else could
And how you did it so easy going
we've never understood.
You accepted the challenge and you
really passed the test,
And when it comes to bosses you're
certainly one of the best.
Whatever happens common sense
you'll always use,
And not a single time your position
you've tried to abuse.
You are straightforward in whatever
you say or do,

And all of us here at Treadwell have
great respect for you.
You are tall timber in the great
field of education,
And the whole thing can be made
in this summation;
Principals may come and great
principals may go,
But another John Renick the System
will never know.
If I had but one thing to say
to you today,
It would be "God bless and keep you
in a special way,"
For you've shown by not only actions
but deeds
What it takes in this world
in order to succeed.

Treadwell Faculty and Staff

A Tribute to Dr. Joyce Jenson

(Career Ladder 1 Instructor)

The six hours a week in T.I.M.
    was time well spent,
As the Tuesdays and Thursdays
    swiftly came and went.
Your positive attiude, enthusiasm
    and contagious smile,

190

Though we were tired, made it
    all seem worthwhile.
You taught each model with eagerness
    and sincerity so deep,
That we couldn't even nod, let
    alone go to sleep.
Your set and instructional objectives
    were so unique
That more about T.I.M. we all
    felt compelled to seek.
The constant input that was
    engaged in by everyone
Made the learning a breeze and
    we had loads of fun.
You monitored and adjusted and
    got active participation
And inspired the class to have
    good peer relation.
So many of the things we'd been doing
    down through the years
By working hard 'mid crowded situations
    blood, sweat, and tears.
But we picked up many new terms
    and some good points too,
Things that, even though experienced, we'd
    never thought to do.
We learned Bloom's Taxonomy from
    the low to the high
And all the variables we promise
    to retain by and by.
As for closure, we'll verbalize, but
    we won't do one more,
For as soon as you give the word, we're
    walking out of that door.

But have no regrets for you've
    done your job well,
As the results of the test we took
    will surely tell.
In all sincerity, Dr, Jenson, you
    have been just great
And we all want you to know that,
    with us, you really do rate.
So keep that beautiful spirit and
    wonderful sense of humor too,
And our prayers are that God
    will forever bless you.

Service

(For a person leaving for another place or retiring)

You were always there whenever we needed you
To help us do all the things we had to do.
You've been honest, humble, patient and kind,
With the welfare of the church uppermost in your mind.
You gave us comfort many times when we were in despair
By quoting Scriptures to us of which we were most
aware—
Of how we should react in the midst of confusion,
And to never ever draw some hasty conclusion.
Your life reflected love and consideration for everyone.
It has shown in so many things you've said and done.
You were here many times when you were physically
worn out
Because you knew this was what the church was all about.
You visited the sick, the disillusioned and the weak,

And a harsh word to no one we ever heard you speak.
You've moved on to work with other women and men,
And to all of them a helping hand to lend.
It won't always be easy nor all your days be bright,
But just keep on working and doing what is right.
Yes, we'll miss you and will always love and respect you
And from God's Heavenly throne He surely won't reject
you.

A Job Well Done

(For a retiring teacher)

You've given of yourself to hundreds of children or more.
You've touched lives as they were never touched before.
You've given them love, guidance, and often times
protection.
You've tried to lead these little ones in the right direction
To get started on the long tedious journey of life
Because you knew it would be filled with problems and
strife.
You've worked more days than we know feeling bad,
But you always gave to them the very best you had.
You changed many a sad little face to one of joy;
You've settled many arguments for each girl or boy.

Under your supervision, down through the years,
You've soothed many wounds and dried many tears.
You've encountered some difficulties with parents too
And were sometimes so frustrated you didn't know what
to do.

But you kept on going even in the face of disaster
By quietly meditating and talking to the Master.
There were times when you felt that it wasn't worthwhile,
But then there was that innocent look and angelic smile
That made you know this was the job God assigned to you
And this particular job no one else could do.
So now you're retiring with memories both happy and sad,
But have no regrets; for you're one of the best the system
ever had.

This Is Your Life

(A Tribute)

A life of service without the thought of pay,
Given so freely, for years, from day to day.
A spirit so humble and a heart so kind
With the progress of others uppermost in your mind.
Despite many digs and untrue accusations
The whole thing can be made in this summation—
You've had endurance and love, patience and care
With shoulders broad enough others' burdens to share.
You've stood firm and yet you were courageous and kind,
Honest, helpful, understanding, and sober of mind.
This is your life, ——, as we have seen it.
And may God grant you a better life for which to redeem it.

A Tribute

They've given of themselves from day to day
To suffering humanity along the way.
In the face of criticism and sometimes disaster,
They continue to do the work of the Master.
They've smiled many times with heavy hearts within
When things seemed hopeless and they had not a friend.

But in the midst of it all, there was a still small voice
Saying, "Keep on working, you have no choice
If eternal life you intend, some day, to achieve
And from these trials eternally be relieved."
So keep on working even in the face of defeat
And from this life's problems never retreat.

A Farewell to Friends

Working at Treadwell School has been
an experience so great,
for each person in the school
I learned to appreciate.

We've worked together peacefully
for sixteen long years,
and they've been years of joy
mixed with only a few tears.

We put our heads together
and always got the job done,
and many lasting friendships
I'm so proud to have won.

You'll always have a special place
in my heart wherever I go,
and I can look back on the good times we had
when I'm feeling low.

I'll cherish these precious memories
as far from your presence I go,
but there is one thing that
I want each of you to know . . .

And that is . . . if there is anything
you think I can do for you,
just give me a chance; call on me;
I'll be happy to!

If I have offended any one of you
in any way,
please forgive me and continue
to love me, I pray.

I'm proud to say that I have
no ill feelings toward anyone,
my battle here has just been fought
and a victory won.

I know not what courses
my life will now take;
what problems confront me,
or what choices I'll have to make.

I only know that each day of my life
I'll always try
to help someone along the way
and keep my aspirations high.

And walk unfaltering through
some beckoning door
to do some of the things
that I've never done before

But my thoughts will be with you
and my sincere prayers too,
for you have a momentous job
and the children are counting on you.

Eulogy

An area of ground is prepared and a seed is planted.
For weeks, this seed is watered and nutured. Finally, a
little sprig peeks out from inside the earth. The sprig is
delicate and needs constant care.

Quickly, the days pass and the excitement of the little
twig begins to wane. Then all of a sudden, one day, we
see a little bud. The anticipation is reactivated and we
begin to keep a more frequent watch, for we know now
that it won't be too long now until it will burst open.
When that glorious day finally does arrive when that bud
has burst open, revealing the handiwork of God, we see
one of the most beautiful flowers your eyes have beheld.
Its petals glimmering in the morning dew or in the cool
refreshing shade of the evening make you realize that
this is a gift that only God could give—one to admire,
touch, and enjoy the sweet aroma and finally pluck at
the height of that beauty. It must be plucked now because
you realize that the little flower will soon begin to close
up, wilt, dry out, and die.

A human life can be compared to this flower. The seed is planted. There is much joy and planning when we learn that the seed is growing. We anxiously share the news with relatives and friends. As the days turn into weeks and the weeks into months, the excitement wears off. All of a sudden, the months have passed and time for deliverance has arrived and our excitement is rekindled. The anticipation is so great that we can hardly maintain our calm.

Then the news comes—it's a boy or it's a girl. We are so thrilled about this bundle of joy that we want the world to know. Announcements are sent out. You and your family and friends are ecstatic with joy. Every time we look at the child, we are reminded that this is God's gift for you to hold, love, and take care of.

You watch this child move from the morning of its life to the noonday or young adulthood, then on to the evening or old age. As each stage develops, the life becomes more beautiful.

In the meantime, the life, like the flower, encountered cold days, delicate times, and many stormy nights. All too soon, we so often feel, that beautiful face that caused so many admiring stares, who brought so much happiness to others and gave so much, begins to wrinkle—the spring, the bounce become careful, uncertain steps. The hair that was once a beautiful coal black, begins to turn first to a silvery gray and then snowy white. The eyes that once sparkled with mischief are now becoming dim, and the mind that was so sharp, functions spasmodically now.

Both lives brought joy, love, and happiness to others. They both served their purpose here on this earth. Both lives were truly worth the living.

PART FIVE

MISCELLANEOUS POETRY

Listen to My Side

Yes, I'm black and proud of it too,
But remember, I have feelings just like you.
Like yours, when you are cut, my blood runs red,
And I too have ambitions, in life to get ahead.

I have mixed emotions at times about other races,
And wonder why they place so much emphasis on the
color of faces.
The same intelligence you have, was granted to me,
Even though we might go about things a little differently.

When you're in need, I don't think of your skin,
For it matters not who you are or where you've been.
All I know is that something within makes me come to
your rescue
And do everything in my power to bring relief to you.

I have the capacity to love every race on earth,
For it was instilled in me by my parents from birth.
Yes, I make mistakes in many things I do and say,
But never would I put a stumbling block in your way.

My heart goes out to you when things in your life go wrong
Because I realize, if I keep living, it won't be too long
Before those same problems or others will knock at my
door
Or some type of life's troubles which we all abhor.

The texture of my skin and hair is different, 'tis true,
But it looks just the way God intended it to.
The bones in my body, like yours, are the same amount.
So is my whole anatomy, including my blood count.

I complain as you do, I rejoice and at times shed tears.
Many things we have in common—our hopes and fears.
I try so very hard to be a good sport,
And only ask for a fair shake in the courts.

I don't want special favours just because it's me,
I just want the fairness in life that was meant to be.
I have my faults and yes, I have my pride,
But none of these things, from you, I've tried to hide.

At times, my very soul is in the basement of despair,
Longing for the peace that God would have us share.
Don't feel, by any means, that I'm just being unkind,
Because I put some of these things on your mind.

I simply want you to pause and give it a thought
Of all the great things on this earth that could be wrought,
And how wonderful it would be if we all worked together,
Come clouds, or sunshine, or winds or stormy weather.

So don't let the fact that I'm black cause you alarm,
Because, in no way, would I do you any harm.

A Challenge—A Chance

Black History Month presents a challenge and gives us
the chance
Our knowledge of the great blacks in history to enhance.
Of the noble accomplishments made down through the
years,
Many made through heartache, blood, sweat and tears.
Of men like Booker T. Washington, Frederick Douglass,
and Martin Luther King,
Whose sincere desire was to truly let freedom ring.
To ring for the young, the old, the black and white,
And set the world an example in terms of what is right.
Many others played their part who are too numerous to
mention,
But their pioneer works should never evade our attention.
Yes, they accepted the challenge and performed works so
grand
That for their greatness we must always take a stand.
The challenge is still being thrown out to each of you,
And there is something we all as Americans can do—
Accept the challenge and take the chances offered you,
And make of them a foundation solid and strong.
Stand up for right and speak out against the wrong
That would obstruct your dream and destroy your plan,
To let the world know that one's color does not make the
man.

February Rap

Listen to a story that we want to tell,
About the month of February that we know so well.
It's a fabulous month that we like so much,
With birthdays of presidents, Valentine and such.
It's the month of Black History and Dental Health,
Just filled to the brim with educational wealth.
The month of American Music and Brotherhood too
The month that gives us so much to do.
So come take a stroll down memory lane,
And learn about some people who brought us fame.
Washington was the father of our country, you know
And Abraham Lincoln helped to make it grow
To the land of the free, a mighty fine nation.
Then Chinese New Year is another celebration.
Marion Anderson and Lindbergh in this month were born,
And the first Boy Scout's uniform was worn.
Susan B. Anthony was a woman so great,
Frederick Douglass was a man that we appreciate.
Dr. Martin Luther King was a mighty fine man,
Who prayed for peace all over this land.
We could go on and on about great men of old,
Who did so many things this country to mold,
But it would take just a little too long,
So we'll stop right here and let the program go on.

A Daily Challenge

Happy faces, sad faces, faces confused as
can be,
Sit day in and day out staring back
at me.
Faces exhibiting grief and some creased
with pain
While I trudge along their confidence
trying to gain.
Faces eager to learn what's in store
for the day,
Faces impatient to go running out of doors
to play.
Faces filled with wonder, faces filled
with cheer,
Faces marked with trouble and lined
sometimes with fear.
Faces filled with sunshine faces
radiant with joy,
Each angelic in its own little way be it
girl or boy.
I study these faces daily with
interest so sincere.
I try hard to erase the frowns and replace
them with cheer.
It isn't always easy to calm the
storms and strife
That somehow have engulfed each
short little life.
I try constantly to do everything
on my part
To bring peace to these faces and joy
into their hearts.

And they respond daily, each in his
very own way
To the love I offer them without the
thought of pay.
It isn't always easy to succeed
in reaching them,
For many are used to getting their
every little whim.
Then many are slow to respond, seeming
sort of wary of me,
For they are wrongly blamed and given
the third degree
By folk much older, but a lot
less understanding,
Too self-righteous, forgetful, obnoxious
and demanding.
Too oft we completely forget the pains of
our own childhood
When we often felt hurt and
totally misunderstood,
When we felt lost and that no one
really cared
And that our interests and problems
no one shared.
These little faces are just carbon
copies of me,
Though a little more active and
mischievous to a degree.
So I pray for the wisdom that only
love can give
To make these little faces really wake
up and live—
I mean living in the sense of giving
all that I can

To help them reach their intellectual zenith to
meet life's demands.

Children

Working with children, I've learned so very much,
For each one, in some special way, I've tried to touch.
Many of them I did reach, but some I did not,
But I've given my best to each and every tot.
I've heard them argue and play then fuss and fight,
And tried very hard many times to decide who was right.
Then in a short spell, regardless of what was done,
I've watched them embrace one another and have lots of
fun.
I've punished them at times for things they did wrong,
And put them back in a child's place where they belong.
Yet, in spite of these disagreements, misunderstandings,
and such,
They've shown in so many ways they love me very much.
I've seen smart ones, slow ones, and some who tried to
cheat,
Then I've seen them draw into a shell and retreat.
I've seen them untidy, even dirty, but most of the times
clean,
But never have I seen one who was just plain mean.
I'm speaking in the sense of adults where they hold a
grudge
And other children's characters try hard to smudge.
They've expressed their love in so very many ways
And shared with me their problems on so many days.
I've seen how objectively they can look at things

As they run around gaily letting their happy laughter
ring.
I've learned from them humbleness, faith, and trust,
And that forgiving and forgetting in this life is a must.
Yes, I've learned many things from the children I've
taught
And the education I received, with money cannot be
bought.

Don't Shed Tears for Me

Weep not for me, dear ones, when
    from this earth I've gone.
Hang not your head in sadness,
    for I walk not alone.
There is someone guiding me every
    step of the way,
The same one who walked and talked
    with me every day.
I have no regrets about going to eternally
    be with others
Who've gone on ahead, I even have
    a wonderful brother
Who's beckoning me and on his face
    is a great big smile
Because he loves me and has been awaiting
    me for a long long while.
Don't shed tears just because
    I've vacated this world,
For I know without a doubt the joys
    that await me are unfurled.

Just try to remember all the blessings
        in life we enjoyed together
And how we stuck by one another mid
        sunshine or cloudy weather.
Think, think about that great day when
        you shall join me
And your soul, too, from this old world
        will be set free.

Tennessee

OH, GREAT, WONDERFUL, BEAUTIFUL
TENNESSEE,
WITH YOUR FIELDS AND TOWERS.
GARDENS AND FLOWERS,
YOU ARE THE ONLY STATE FOR ME.
IN WAR AND PEACE, YOU KNEW WHAT TO DO.
HOME FOR DAVY CROCKETT AND THREE
PRESIDENTS, TOO.
MY, I AM PROUD OF YOU!
KNOWN NOT ONLY FOR COTTON, WOOD AND
CORN,
BUT ALSO YOU ARE THE STATE WHERE THE
BLUES WAS BORN.
YOU ARE THE VOLUNTEER STATE, SO GRAND
AND FREE,
WITH THE MIGHTY MISSISSIPPI AND THE
SMOKIES FOR ALL TO SEE.

Your natural resources are too numerous to mention,
But I would like to bring these to your attention.
Your soil so rich, I like to boast,
And futhermore, there is no coast.

On your forests, climate, and water I rely;
And also on the marble, zinc, and coal you supply
Yes, you are the greatest state in all the land,
With the copper, silver, and stone in great demand.
Your industries are many for everyone to see,
So I'll pause a minute while everyone listens to me.
Chemical manufactures, textiles, and food products too;
Yes, TENNESSEE, you'll more than just do!
Dairies help you rate,
As a leading state.
Your coal mines produce millions of tons per year,
Yet in your forests, roam wild rabbits and deer.
Beautiful tulip poplar trees
Bow in the breeze.
Your stately iris flowers
Withstand the showers.
You stretch from North Carolina to Arkansas,
You enforce our government with the law.
Yes, Indians once roamed your forests and hills,
Hunting food and curing ills.
Your state bird, the mockingbird,
Sings the loveliest tunes you ever heard.
Your forests and state parks
Are homes for great landmarks.
Even though the Civil War tore you apart,
You worked hard for a new start.
Through the bad times and the good times too,
Tennessee, I dearly love you.

The Beauty of Youth

Ah, for the burning flame of youth
    When the body knows no pain,
When even a sigh can be a melody
    And every word a sweet refrain.
When even gray skies dull not the spirit
    of beauty come what may
And just being alive is super and
    wondrous experiences arise every day.
When hatred has not invaded the heart
    nor jealousy, nor trouble nor strife,
Just having a zest for living each moment
    and getting the very best out of life.

Growing Old

I've often wondered just why do we have
    to grow old,
I have to wonder because this is something
    I'd never been told.
Why can't we stay young and innocent
    happy and gay?
Sometimes I wish that it could always
    be this way.
Then I thought to myself—why, that
    would never do,
For I'd never know as many things,
    Mom, as you.
I wouldn't be able to have a family and
    work like Dad.

Then I'd never understand why many times
        grownups are so sad.
When I think about it, I guess growing old
        really isn't that bad,
So I'll just have all the fun I can
        while I'm a lad.

Wonders of Nature

As the gentle wind softly whispers
through the trees
And beautiful butterflies flutter about
enjoying the breeze,
The babbling brook just continues to
flow lazily along
And overhead the birds fly past
singing their song;
As the old owl sits perched on
some limb a-hooting
And mischievous boys rush by on
their bikes a-scooting,
As the lovely sky all decked in colors
of blue and white
Fades away as Mother Nature
prepares for the night,
Just watching all these things brings
joy to my heart,
For I know, without a doubt, where
each one got its start.
Then I think to myself, how
insignificant am I,
But I'm just thankful to God for
letting me pass by.

Snow

When the grounds in winter are all dressed in white,
And the moon gives off a sharp but peaceful light,
Its beauty is really something to see
And a reminder that it could but come, dear God, from
Thee.
Its loveliness seems on each of us to cast a spell,
Upon everything it touches and everyone as well.
In spite of its beauty, it can bring a whole city to a stop,
And cause power failures and tree limbs to drop.
It can slow down the traffic almost to crawl,
And close schools, businesses, jobs and all.
Yes, snow is beautiful but it's powerful too.
But I really do love the snow, don't you?

Snow Is Falling

Snow is falling, gently falling—falling
all over the town,
No matter where we go and look,
it's swiftly falling down.
Down on the tree tops covering
every cranny and nook,
Snow is falling, gently falling
everywhere you look.
It's falling on the courthouse, it's
falling on the steeple
It's falling gently falling—falling
on all the people.

Fall

Fall is a season whose beauty we can
    enjoy with ease,
As we watch the beautiful leaves gently
    falling from the trees.
They seem to be preparing for winter
    by getting undressed,
For they know that by the north wind they'll
    soon be possessed.
They all soon become bare except
    for the evergreen,
For it's determined that winter won't
    destroy its scene.
And when the snow falls upon it and
    the green turns to white,
It's one of Mother Nature's most
    endearing sights.
I like the spring, I like the summer
    and the fall,
Because there's something special about each
    and I like them all.

March

I

The wind is high, the trees are sighing,
    the ground is soaking wet;
On the streets, paper and hats are flying,
    But the mood'll change by noon, I'll bet.
Kites are flying way up into the sky
    While happy children frolic about,
Sleepy flowers peek out from wherever they lie,
    You'd better have fun while the sun is out!

II

The blue bird is singing a merry song,
    The wren, the jay and the robin too,
The water in the brook flows lazily along
    And the sky is a beautiful azure blue.
The trees are budding, the shrubbery turning green,
    The blading grass begins to peek,
Wondering if it's time to come on the scene
    Or if old March is just playing hide and seek.

III

The bees are buzzing every now and then,
    Butterflies decide to try their wings.
Mother bear brings her cubs out of the den,
    And the children's laughter gaily rings.
The clouds roll around the sky playing games
    With the weather vane atop the gate.
We know without a doubt old March is here
    And we'll have to accept her fate.

The Beauty of Spring

Of all the wonderful seasons,
I'd surely choose spring,
With budding trees, flowers blooming,
and grass so bright and green.
With insects awakening and soft breezes
gently kissing my face
And dainty clouds moving about,
never staying in one place.
The homely moth changes into
a beautiful butterfly,
With laughing children flying kites
high up in the sky.
The ground begins to soften, yielding
many hibernating creatures
From the long chill of winter with
their peculiar features.
Cardinals, sparrows, robins, and
blue jays too
flitting gaily about in spite of
the morning dew.
Chickadees happily chirping, daffodils
beginning to peek,
For they too like spring and its
wondeful aroma to seek.
Spring is the season that by so
many is treasured,
Because its true beauty in no way
can be measured.

Spring

Spring is here, what pleasure
what joy
To every happy girl and every
dashing boy.
It's a time when children can have
lots of fun
With nothing to do but frolic,
rip and run.
To spread a tent out by the old
oak tree,
And chase after every butterfly
and bumblebee,
To fly their kites and on their
scooters skate
Up and down the sidewalks and back
through the gates.
Time for dinner, you'll hear
someone shout
Then boy, what scrambling and
rushing about!
To get to the face bowl and wash
hands and faces,
Then get to the table to take
their places.
Dinner is soon over, now it's time
for rest,
This is the time they all seem
to detest.